# Workbook

T0392214

Melanie Starren

CAMBRIDGE
UNIVERSITY PRESS

# Map of the book

| | Vocabulary | Grammar | Cross-curricular | Skills |
|---|---|---|---|---|
| **1 In style**<br>Mission: Write a review<br>Page 4 | Clothes<br>Parts of clothes<br>**Pronunciation:**<br>Plural pronunciation of "s" | **Comparative adjectives, adverbs, and** *as … as*<br>*On the first site, the shoes were much more expensive.*<br>*I took the T-shirt out of the box as quickly as I could.*<br>**The simple present with future meaning**<br>*The bus leaves at 6:15.* | **Clothes throughout history**<br>Learn about clothes and materials in the past, present, and future. | **Literature**<br>*King Canute's day on the beach*<br>A story<br>Speaking<br>Reading and Writing<br>Listening |
| **2 Future technology**<br>Mission: Recommend new technology<br>Page 16 | Technology<br>Verbs for using computers<br>**Pronunciation:**<br>Syllable stress in two-syllable words | **The first conditional**<br>*If my mom says it's OK, then I'll go.*<br>**The zero and first conditional**<br>*If the floor is dirty, a robot drives around and cleans.*<br>*If I'm hungry, I'll ask the freezer, "What ice cream do we have?"* | **How to make an app**<br>Learn what an app is and what you need to make one. | **Literature**<br>*The IAST Times*<br>A newspaper article<br>Speaking<br>Reading and Writing |
| **Review units 1–2** | | | | |
| **3 Jim-nastics**<br>Mission: Invent a new sport<br>Page 30 | Sports<br>Activities, games, people, and equipment<br>**Pronunciation:**<br>Contracted forms | **The passive (simple present)**<br>*Dog surfing competitions are organized by people all around the world.*<br>**Modal verbs**<br>*Birch may have made a mistake.*<br>*This could be the most important point today.*<br>*The ball might go into the net!*<br>*Can we watch that goal again?* | **How athletes prepare for sport**<br>Learn how athletes train, eat, and sleep before competitions. | **Literature**<br>*The Spartan Princess*<br>A comic book<br>Reading and Writing<br>Listening |
| **4 Be careful!**<br>Mission: Find out about emergency services<br>Page 42 | Accidents and illnesses<br>Health and medicine<br>**Pronunciation:**<br>Sentence stress | **The present perfect with** *how long*, *for,* **and** *since*<br>*I haven't been well for a week.*<br>*She's had a problem with her heart since April.*<br>**The present progressive for future plans**<br>*We're taking her to the vet this evening.* | **Changes in medicine**<br>Learn about vaccinations and treatments. | **Literature**<br>*The $20,000 adventure*<br>A story<br>Listening |
| **Review units 3–4** | | | | |
| **5 Fun foods**<br>Mission: Take part in a cooking competition<br>Page 56 | Cooking ingredients<br>Cooking actions and equipment<br>**Pronunciation:**<br>Intonation in questions | *Rather* **and** *prefer*<br>*I prefer carrots to broccoli.*<br>*I'd rather have salmon.*<br>**The passive (simple past)**<br>*The sandwich wasn't made from bread.*<br>*It was made from two cookies and some ice cream.* | **Food groups**<br>Learn about why some foods are good for you. | **Literature**<br>*The very, very interesting journal of Juana Sánchez*<br>A journal<br>Speaking<br>Listening<br>Reading and Writing |

| | | Vocabulary | Grammar | Cross-curricular | Skills |
|---|---|---|---|---|---|
| 6 | **Environmentally friendly**<br>Mission: Share ideas to protect your environment!<br>Page 68 | Home<br>The environment<br>**Pronunciation:**<br>Word stress | ***A lot of, lots of, a few, a little, many, much***<br>*There's a lot of water from our town's river.*<br>*There are lots of fish living in the water.*<br>*Many people don't believe me.*<br>*My house doesn't use much electricity.*<br>*There's a little milk in the fridge.*<br>*We only throw away a few bags each year.*<br><br>**Tag questions**<br>*Everyone recycles a lot, don't they?*<br>*You couldn't recycle, could you?* | **Ecosystems in the city**<br>Learn about the animals that make their home in the city. | **Literature**<br>***The fall of a Mayan city***<br>A story<br><br>Speaking<br>Reading and Writing |
| | **Review units 5–6** | | | | |
| 7 | **Feeling it**<br>Mission: Make a "feelings wheel"<br>Page 82 | Feelings and emotions<br>Well-being<br>**Pronunciation:**<br>"Wh" questions | ***Don't need to, have to, should, shouldn't, ought to***<br>*I have to wait until I'm older.*<br>*If your parents say you can't have a snake, you have to listen to them!*<br>*You should not get a snake without telling your parents!*<br>*You don't need to worry if some of your ideas aren't very good.*<br>*You should try to be satisfied with what you have.*<br>*You ought to write about something you love.*<br><br>***Such ... that / so ... that***<br>*It's so much fun that my mom and I always laugh a lot!*<br>*It's such a relaxing place that I once fell asleep there!* | **Emotional awareness**<br>Learn about empathy and how we show emotions. | **Literature**<br>***The cowboy who cried wolf***<br>A story<br><br>Speaking<br>Reading and Writing<br>Listening |
| 8 | **Pretty cities**<br>Mission: Plan a city visit<br>Page 94 | A tour of a city<br>Visiting new places<br>**Pronunciation:**<br>Intonation in questions | **Indirect questions**<br>*Do you know how many paintings there are?*<br><br>***Used to / didn't use to***<br>*They used to make the air very dirty.*<br>*Today the trains are electric, but they didn't use to be.* | **Responsible tourism**<br>Learn how to take care of places when you go on vacation. | **Literature**<br>***The case of the Butterfly Diamond***<br>A novel<br><br>Speaking<br>Reading and Writing<br>Reading |
| | **Review units 7–8** | | | | |
| 9 | **Lights, camera, action!**<br>Mission: Make a scene for a movie or TV show<br>Page 108 | TV and movie genres<br>Television<br>**Pronunciation:**<br>Word stress | **Causative *have/get***<br>*Mom's having a special superhero cake made for me.*<br><br>**The second conditional**<br>*If I had $250 million, I'd buy cameras and costumes for the actors.* | **Special effects**<br>Learn how special effects are used in movies. | **Literature**<br>***The Monster in our Homes!***<br>A poem<br><br>Speaking<br>Reading and Writing<br>Writing |
| 10 | **Review Unit**<br>Page 120 | Units 1–9 | Units 1–9 | | |

3

# 1 In style

## My goal

**I can have a simple conversation about a topic I know.** 5

**Mission Complete!**

**I can find important information in simple texts.** 3

**I can read and understand schedules and opening times.** 4

**I can understand the main points and some details from a short passage.** 2

**I can understand about clothes when I read a text.** 1

**And I need ...**

**To do this, I will ...**

**So I can ...**

**I want to practice ...**

 **Diary**

What I already know about clothes and style ...

What I have learned about clothes and style ...

## 1 Match the letters to the same color. Make words and label the pictures.

| t | swea | at | je | sw | rai |
|---|------|----|----|----|-----|
| s | e | nco | ui | i | t |
| ims | uit | wel | uit | ry | ts |

 **1**    **2**    **3**   **4**    **5**    **6**

1 _raincoat_

## 2 Read and complete with the correct words.

Hey, Sara. Have you heard about what Renata did at the school party?

> Oh, no. What's she done now, Lucas? 😕

Well, as usual she wanted to make everyone laugh, so she wore her mom's long cream ¹ _raincoat_ and then under that …

> Shorts and T-shirt? Hawaiian shirt? Ice cream costume? 😊

It was worse! She was wearing the same clothes as Mrs. Perkins! She had a pair of blue ² _____ with gold spots. She also wore a short pink skirt and a yellow patterned ³ _____.

> Ha ha! Mrs. Perkins always wears bright things. Was Renata cold?

Not really. On top of her yellow top, she had a nice warm orange ⁴ _____. And you know how Mrs. Perkins loves colorful rings, earrings, and bracelets?

> Yes, she loves all sorts of ⁵ _____.

Well, Renata wore a huge ring on EVERY finger!

> Awesome. And let me guess, she carried a big ⁶ _____ on her arm, and on her feet, she had those green and white ⁷ _____ that Mrs. Perkins wears to school.

That's right. And do you know the best thing? Well, when Mrs. Perkins walked in and saw Renata …

## 3 🎧 5.02 Listen and answer. Write *yes* or *no*.

1 Mrs. Perkins was angry with Renata.

2 Mrs. Perkins was wearing old jeans.

3 Lucas thinks Mrs. Perkins was sad.

**1** **Read the text.** Find and complete the adjectives.

1 w e l l  k n o w n

2 h _ _ _ _ y

3 a _ _ _ _ _ _ e

4 c _ _ _ _ p

5 t _ _ _ _ _ _ d

6 d _ _ _ y

# WHO'S YOUR FAVORITE CLOTHES DESIGNER?

## Valeria

My favorite designer is Anaya Acharya. Have you heard of her? She's from India and she's very well known in her country. She was only seven years old when she started to design clothes. She was always in trouble in school because instead of doing her school work, she drew clothes! I don't think her teachers were very happy with her. But she's now in fashion school and was the youngest designer in international fashion week last year. I really want to buy one of her dresses – they're awesome!

## Grace

Do you know the Olsen twins, Mary-Kate and Ashley? They're actors, but I think they're better at designing clothes. They make clothes for girls. They sell their clothes in supermarkets. The clothes are cheap, so I can buy T-shirts and jeans with my own money. They also make purses and jewelry and they've won a lot of prizes. They're very talented.

## Santiago

My favorite designer isn't famous (yet!) and you can't buy his clothes in stores. His name is Greg Nelson and he went to school with my brother. He takes all kinds of old clothes that nobody wants, like dirty old sweaters, sweatsuits, and even suits and ties and makes them into clothes for young people who don't have anywhere to live. He thinks it's important that everyone can wear clothes that make them feel good, and I agree. He's my hero!

**2** ⭐ **Read the text again and answer the questions.**

1 Who has two favorite designers? _____

2 Who likes someone who lives in a different country? _____

3 Who has a family member who is the same age as his/her favorite designer? _____

4 Who wants to buy something by his/her favorite designer? _____

5 Who owns something by his/her favorite designer? _____

6 Who has the same opinion as his/her favorite designer? _____

## ★ Grammar: comparative adjectives, adverbs, and *as ... as*

**1** **Choose the correct answer.**

1 Paula can run **as quick as** / (**more quickly**) in her new sneakers. Her new ones are the right size.

2 My old purse was very big. My new purse **isn't as small as** / **is smaller than** my old purse.

3 Dad's new tie is **as ugly as** / **uglier than** his old tie! He always buys ugly ties!

4 The jewelry is a lot **less expensive** / **more expensive** in this store. The jewelry in the other store was very expensive.

5 This swimsuit **isn't as big as** / **is bigger than** that swimsuit. That one's smaller.

6 Please move **more closely** / **closer** to your brother for the picture.

**2** **Complete the sentences with the correct form of the words in the box.**

> bad    good    ~~friendly~~    hot    interesting    nice

1 Sam is ___friendlier___ than his brother. His brother never says "Hi".

2 Which subject do you find _____ : English, science, or history?

3 Bananas are _____ than oranges. I don't really like oranges.

4 I'm _____ than you at math. I always get As.

5 Australia is _____ than the U.K. It's 40 degrees in Melbourne today.

6 Katy isn't good at skiing, but she's even _____ at snowboarding. She can't stand on a snowboard!

**3** **Look and write the differences.** Use the correct form of the words in the box. Then write two more sentences.

> angry    brave    cold
> ~~happy~~    tall

Elif is happier than Yesim. _____

_____

_____

_____

_____

**1** **Look, read, and complete the sentences.**

1 a small, green button from my favorite jacket

2 the c_____r on my new shirt

3 my new c_____n I got for my birthday

4 the l_____r sofa in my living room

5 the p_____n on my school skirt

6 the l_____l inside my favorite jeans

**2** **Look at Clara's online scrapbook.** Order the letters and complete the messages.

SEARCH

This is my uncle eating a hot dog. He got tomato ketchup on his **lksi** _____ tie.

This is my brother. He's five in this picture. He liked painting then. There's paint on his **levsees** _____.

These are my new sneakers. I'm a **zies** _____ 4 now! I love them.

This is my favorite picture. It's a scarf and it's made of **nottco** _____! Isn't it colorful?

I went to a costume party last week. I **edtir no** _____ lots of costumes, but this was what I wore.

**3** **Choose one more picture from Clara's online scrapbook and write a message.**

This is a … It's made of …

It's wearing … It has …

## ★ Grammar: simple present with future meaning

### 1 Choose the correct answer.

1 Jack's party **begins** / **begin** at 2 p.m. on Saturday afternoon. Wear something colorful!

2 The school bus **leaving** / **leaves** in three minutes. Run!

3 Our school vacation **don't start** / **doesn't start** in June next year. It starts in July.

4 Dinner at Grandma's **isn't** / **be** at 8 p.m. tomorrow. It's at 7 p.m. today. Don't be late!

### 2 Read and complete the sentences.

**Sebastian's Shoes**
9:00–5:30
Monday, Tuesday,
Wednesday, Friday
9:00–7:00 Thursday
10:00–6:00 Saturday

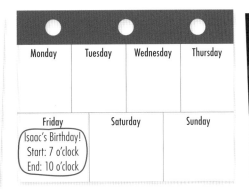

| Monday | Tuesday | Wednesday | Thursday |
|---|---|---|---|
| Friday | Saturday | Sunday | |

Isaac's Birthday!
Start: 7 o'clock
End: 10 o'clock

*COSMO THE
CLOWN'S CIRCUS –
HERE TOMORROW!*
Fun for Families
North Street Park
2 p.m., 4 p.m., 7 p.m.
90 minutes long

1 It's 7 a.m. on Monday morning. Sebastian's store _____ in two hours.

2 Isaac's party _____ at 10 p.m.

3 The first show _____ at 2 p.m. tomorrow.

## Speaking 🎤

### 3 ▶ Ezgi and Pablo are doing some speaking practice. Watch and write *Ezgi* or *Pablo*.

1 Who gives more than one answer for some questions? _____

2 Who <u>doesn't</u> use adjectives to make their answers interesting? _____

3 Who do you think gives better answers?
_____

**PRONUNCIATION TIP!** The letter "s" can often sound like a /z/ at the end of plural words.

### 4 In pairs, read, and make Pablo's answers more interesting.

| | |
|---|---|
| **Teacher:** | Who do you go with? |
| **Pablo:** | My friends. |
| **Teacher:** | Where do you go on weekends with your friends? |
| **Pablo:** | To the movies. |
| **Teacher:** | Anywhere else? |
| **Pablo:** | There's a sports center. |

**SPEAKING TIP!** Try not to give yes/no answers.

**1** **Read the story and order the sentences.**

_____ The king told the sea not to get his clothes wet.

___1___ King Canute's servants thought that he had special powers.

_____ So, he went to the beach with his servants.

_____ Because it didn't listen to him, he got very wet.

_____ The sea didn't listen to the king.

_____ He wanted to teach them that he wasn't as powerful as they thought.

**2** **Read and answer.** Write *yes* or *no*.

1 The servants gave King Canute a fish on a silver dish.     no

2 The fruit was in an enormous bowl.

3 King Canute usually wears a silk shirt, a suit, and a crown.

4 King Canute took his throne to the beach.

5 The servants followed the king to the beach.

6 King Canute has superpowers and didn't get wet.

**3** **Read, match, and write.**

**1** To keep him dry when he's in the sea, the king might wear an …

**a**

**2** The king usually wears an expensive …

**b**         orange raincoat  1

**3** When the king climbs the castle as fast as a spider, I think he always wears unusual …

**c**

**4** It gets cold living in a castle, so I think the king likes to wear his large …

**d**

**4** ⭐ **Fill in the blanks.**

A funny thing happened this morning. I put the king's clothes in his bedroom for him as usual, but

he wanted ¹_____to_____ wear his jeans, not his suit! I think his suit is much nicer ²_____ his

jeans! Then, the king went to the beach and he asked us to go ³_____ him.

We ⁴_____ his throne to the edge of the water. That throne is ⁵_____ heavy as a very

big dinner table! Then, he ⁶_____ down on his throne by the sea! He told the sea not to wet his

clothes. But it did, of course. The king got very wet, and we all got very wet, ⁷_____ .

**5** **In pairs, write what happened next.** Complete the sentences.

King Canute was very wet so he went back to the castle to change his clothes.

Then, he _____ .

It was lunchtime and he was hungry.

But there was _____ .

The servant said, "No, I'm not going to bring you that! The sea didn't listen to you, so I'm not going to!"

The king was very _____ .

After lunch and wearing his crown on his head, but not his wet cloak, he went to his study.

He was thinking about _____ .

**1** **Read the text again and answer the questions.**

1   Which natural materials did people in the Middle Ages use to make clothes?

_____

2   Why do people like man-made textiles?

_____

3   What is fleece made from?

_____

4   Why is fleece good?

_____

5   What can smart textiles do?

_____

**2** **Find examples of these materials and complete the chart.**

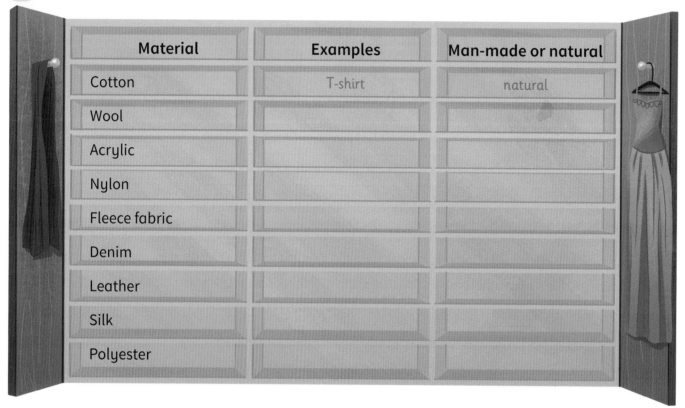

| Material | Examples | Man-made or natural |
| --- | --- | --- |
| Cotton | T-shirt | natural |
| Wool | | |
| Acrylic | | |
| Nylon | | |
| Fleece fabric | | |
| Denim | | |
| Leather | | |
| Silk | | |
| Polyester | | |

**3** **Write about and draw the type of clothes you think we will be wearing in the future.**

In the future, clothes will _____

hot weather    cold weather

**1** For these questions, choose the correct answer.

**1**

Pedro, text me after the movie.
We're too late and can't get tickets.
See you back at Laura's house.
Steve

**What does Steve want Pedro to do?**

- **A** Meet him at Laura's house.
- **B** Get tickets for him.
- **C** Wait for him inside the movie theater.

**2**

Natalie,
Your cousin has lost his gold chain. Did you see it in the bathroom yesterday? If you find it, give him a call.
Mom

- **A** Mom is telling Natalie to look in the bathroom.
- **B** Mom has lost Natalie's gold chain.
- **C** Natalie should telephone her cousin if she finds the jewelry.

**3**

Aunt Mary,
The competition is this weekend, but the swimsuit Dad bought me is at his house. Can you ask him to give it to Charlie?
Alice.

**What's Alice's problem?**

- **A** She doesn't have her swimsuit.
- **B** Charlie has her swimsuit.
- **C** Her dad needs to buy her a new swimsuit.

**4**

### Special offer on all sneakers sizes 4–8.
This Monday only.
From 9 a.m.–noon.

- **A** All sneakers will be cheaper on Monday morning.
- **B** Some sneakers will be cheaper every day except Monday morning.
- **C** You can buy some sneakers at a special price on Monday morning.

**5**

Dave,
Your suit and tie are at the cleaner's on Bright Street. Please go there after lunch, but remember the store closes at 5 p.m.
Patty

**What does Dave have to do?**

- **A** Take his suit and tie to the cleaner's.
- **B** Pick up his suit and tie before 5 p.m.
- **C** Meet Patty at the cleaner's after lunch.

**6**

**"Snack Times"!**
Tomato and olive or red pepper bread.
Delicious with cheese! $1.50 per bag.

- **A** There are three types of snacks.
- **B** A bag of cheese costs $1.50.
- **C** You can eat this snack with cheese.

My progress: /6

**1** 🎧 5.03 **Listen.** For each question, choose the correct picture.

**1** How many children went to the fashion show?

A ☐

B ☐

C ☐

**2** What food will the children make?

A ☐

B ☐

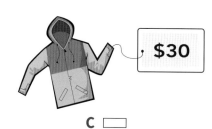

C ☐

**3** How much is the raincoat?

A ☐

B ☐

C ☐

**4** What will the weather be like when Paul goes out?

A ☐

B ☐

C ☐

**5** What will the girl try on?

A ☐

B ☐

C ☐

**6** Which factory did Jim visit last year?

A ☐

B ☐

C ☐

My progress: ☐ /6

## 1 Read and complete the sentences.

1  My sneakers are size 4. My shoes are size 5. (small)

   My sneakers are _____ my shoes.

2  A zebra runs at 64 km/hr. An elephant runs at 40 km/hr. (slow)

   An elephant runs _____ a zebra.

3  Gael got 91% in math. Maria got 94% in math. (good)

   Maria is _____ Gael at math.

4  Thomas is scared of spiders. Ben isn't scared of spiders. (brave)

   Thomas isn't _____ as Ben.

## 2 Order the words to make sentences.

1  movie / The / starts / 2 p.m. / at

   _____

2  leaves / bus / at / 5:14. / The

   _____

3  work / finishes / Kieron / at / today / 4 p.m.

   _____

4  My / at / class / 12:00. / ends

   _____

5  The / game / begins / lunch. / after / soccer

   _____

## 3 Complete the sentences with the clothes words.

1  I don't want a p a t t e r n. No spots and no stripes, please.

2  What __i__ do you want to try on? Small or medium?

3  Matt works in a bank. He always wears a ___i__ and tie to work.

4  You look cold. Here – put on my s ___t__ r.

5  Look – it's on the ___b___. "Made in Spain, 100 % cotton."

6  I'm going on vacation tomorrow. Do you like my new __w___s____?

## 4 In pairs, answer the questions.

Describe what someone in the class is wearing.　Florencia is wearing a …

Make comparative sentences with *carefully*, *fast*, *boring*, and *badly*.　I draw more …

Find a label in your clothes. What does it say?　It says …

What time does your next class start? What is it?　History starts at …

# 2 Future technology

## My goal

I can read a newspaper article. **5**

## Mission Complete!

I can decide if sentences about a story are correct. **3**

I can give my opinion. **4**

I can read noticeboards and posters. **2**

I can solve simple puzzles. **1**

What I already know about technology …

What I have learned about technology …

### And I need …

### To do this, I will …

### So I can …

### I want to practice …

**(2)**

**1** **Find the words and label the pictures.**

| V | S | P | Y | X | G | Z | K | G | C | U | O |
|---|---|---|---|---|---|---|---|---|---|---|---|
| M | O | C | O | S | B | C | E | U | P | Y | H |
| O | R | Y | R | B | Y | P | Y | J | R | I | G |
| U | J | C | D | E | R | S | B | T | I | S | M |
| S | K | O | E | I | E | P | O | T | N | A | K |
| E | G | X | N | L | G | N | A | W | T | Q | F |
| M | V | T | W | E | L | M | R | O | E | V | Z |
| T | R | U | T | E | S | P | D | R | R | Z | B |
| R | I | E | F | C | I | H | H | Y | D | X | S |
| H | H | B | S | N | L | M | Y | O | E | I | G |
| L | A | P | T | O | P | D | S | C | N | W | O |
| M | A | U | Y | C | X | H | O | G | V | E | R |

keyboard

**2** **Match the words to the definitions.**

| | | | | |
|---|---|---|---|---|
| **1** | hardware | **a** | instructions or code for a computer |
| **2** | software | **b** | parts of a computer |
| **3** | program | **c** | a thin, round, flat object you put in a computer |
| **4** | disk | **d** | the programs that are used to run a computer |

**3** **Read and complete the text.**

I love my cat, but she's very silly. I'm trying to do my homework on my ¹ _____ right now, but she's playing with the ² _____ , moving it with her nose and her feet. When she sees something she likes on the ³ _____ , a video or something like that, she jumps and tries to hit it. And she also likes the noise the letters make on the ⁴ _____ djso;hgdkjbksjgfieg??? Oh, no – she sat on it. I think I'll give her an old ⁵ _____ to play with instead.

**4** **Choose a piece of technology and think of a definition.** **In pairs, ask and answer.**

My favorite piece of technology is something you use to ... _____

**1** 🎧 5.04 **Listen and (circle) the words you hear.**

| 1 | reply | message | email | | 3 | playground | bottle | brother |
| 2 | cat | soccer | ball | | 4 | work | expensive | write |

**2** 🎧 5.05 ⭐ **Listen again. For each question, choose the correct picture.**

**1** How did Rafael contact Anna?

A ⬜

B ⬜

C ⬜

**2** Which screen are they using to watch the video?

A ⬜

B ⬜

C ⬜

**3** What are they looking at?

A ⬜

B ⬜

C ⬜

**4** What can Abril borrow?

A ⬜

B ⬜

C ⬜

## ⭐ Grammar: the first conditional

**1** **Complete the sentences with the words in the box.**

> ~~buy~~   isn't   miss   will   will you   won't

1   If I _____ buy _____ a new cell phone, I'll use it every day.
2   If I don't see you tomorrow, I _____ give you a present.
3   If your laptop breaks, _____ buy a new one?
4   Dante _____ give his homework to his teacher if he can use the printer.
5   Kate won't play tennis if it _____ sunny.
6   Will your parents take you to school if you _____ the bus?

**2** **Complete the first conditional sentences with the verbs in parentheses.**

1   If I break my sister's laptop, she _____ 'll be _____ angry. (be)
2   If Ben _____, he won't play for Manchester United. (not practice)
3   If you _____ sick tomorrow, will you stay at home? (be)
4   We'll watch the movie on my laptop if the Internet _____. (work)
5   They _____ to Brazil if they can't get tickets. (not go)
6   Will Agustina _____ me with my homework if I give her chocolate? (help)

**3** **Order the words to make sentences.**

1   the / if / She / won't / there's / a shark. / water / go in

_____

2   will / hurt. / drink / your stomach / too many / If / you / milkshakes

_____

3   be there. / the / won't / on Saturday night / If / he / to / goes / movies / his friends

_____

4   a ticket / don't / travel. / If / you / have / you can't

_____

**4** **In pairs, take turns to say an ending and guess which is the beginning.**

> … I'll build a snowman!    If it snows, you'll build a snowman.    That's right! Your turn!

> If I go to the beach this weekend, …    If you break your leg, …

> If I have some eggs, sugar, butter, and flour, …    If it snows, …

**1** **Read and complete with the correct form of the words in the box.**

> chat   click   download   ~~email~~   enter   install   text   turn off   turn on   upload

Lucy wants you to
¹ _email_ her.
Her address is
lucylou07@email.com.

I ² _____ Paddington 2 last night. We can watch it together!

I can't see you, Samuel.

Oh, Grandma. If you ³ _____ the camera on your laptop, you'll see me!

Oh, yes! Hi, Samuel!

60%

Diego's lost your phone number. Will you ⁴ _____ him if I give you his number? It's (770) 090-0461.

You should NEVER ⁵ _____ on web links you don't know.

What's your brother doing?

He's ⁶ _____ with Vera – AGAIN!

Jimena,
I've told you a million times! ⁷ _____ your laptop and your P.C. when you go to bed!

I want to see your pictures of the party.

OK, OK. I'll ⁸ _____ them now if my sister isn't using the laptop.

Can you ⁹ _____ some games on my new cell phone, please?
If you write your password and press ¹⁰ _____ , your email account will open.

**2** **Write a reply to the messages.** Use the verbs from Activity 1.

Your uncle sent you a birthday present, but you didn't say thank you!

I'm sorry. I'll email him now to say thank you.

Shall we watch a movie tonight?

_____

_____

The light was on in your bedroom all day!

_____

_____

## Grammar: the zero conditional and first conditional

**1** Complete the sentences with the correct form of the verbs in the box. Then circle.

> click   eat   meet   phone

1   If they go to the festival, they _____ Little Mix.       Zero / 1st
2   I _____ this button if I get an email.       Zero / 1st
3   If someone _____ you, your cell phone plays a song.       Zero / 1st
4   James _____ the olives if you put them in his salad.       Zero / 1st

**2** Write zero and first conditional sentences.

1   you / drop a ball / bounce

2   it / snow tomorrow / go snowboarding

3   you / clean your room / give you some money

4   people / not cut their hair / grow

**3** Watch Pablo and Ezgi doing some speaking practice.

**4** Which of the different types of technology do you like best?

**5** Watch the video again. Complete the sentences.

**Pablo:** I like the helicopter. It looks fun.

**Ezgi:** I ¹___agree___. I have a helicopter like this, but it's green. I ²_____ my helicopter at the beach. I really ³_____ the camera, too.

**Pablo:** Really? ⁴_____. It looks like it's for young children.

**Ezgi:** … Do you have a laptop?

**Pablo:** No, I don't, but I can use my brother's laptop. I ⁵_____ my cell phone.

**Teacher:** Do you think taking pictures is fun?

**Pablo:** Yes, I do. I ⁶_____ pictures and then choosing the best ones.

**Ezgi:** I ⁷_____ taking pictures, but I sometimes take pictures on my phone.

> **SPEAKING TIP!** It's important to use a variety of expressions for likes and dislikes.

> **PRONUNCIATION TIP!** In two-syllable words, the stress is usually on the first syllable. In three-syllable words, the stress is usually on the second syllable.

**1** **Read the story from *THE IAST TIMES* and order the sentences.**

_____ Everyone wants to talk about Azra's app.

_____ Dr. Şafak tells the class about the competition.

_____ Burak feels unhappy because he didn't win the competition.

_____ Everyone says Burak is going to win the competition.

_____ Dr. Şafak tells the class that Azra is the winner.

**2** **Read and answer.** Write *yes* or *no*. **In pairs, explain your answers.**

1 Dr. Şafak told students about the competition five weeks ago. _____ no

2 Burak learns about computers at home. _____

3 Nobody thinks Burak is going to win the competition. _____

4 Azra has been at the school for three months. _____

5 Azra loves chatting and talks a lot. _____

6 Burak feels sad when Azra wins the competition. _____

**3** **Azra's app helps students make schedules.** What app would help you in school? Read the example and write your own ideas.

I would like an app to help me practice my spelling. There could be a penguin character that shows me difficult words!

**4** **Burak feels sad when he loses the competition.** Why? In pairs, discuss the three possible reasons (a–c). Then talk about how you would feel in the same situation.

a He thought he was going to win.

b He doesn't believe Azra's app is better than his.

c He is surprised that Azra knows so much about technology.

**5** 🎧 5.06 ⭐ **Listen.** For each question, choose the correct answer.

1 You hear Dr. Şafak talking to her class.

What does she tell her students?

 A What the winner of the competition will win.

 B How to enter the competition.

 C When the competition is going to start.

2 You hear Azra and Burak talking about the competition.

Azra says

 A she hopes Burak will win it.

 B she isn't going to enter the competition.

 C she has a good idea for an app.

3 You hear Dr. Şafak talking to her class.

What does she say about the competition?

 A not many students entered it

 B she didn't have time to look at everybody's app

 C she is happy with the work the students did

4 You hear Azra and Burak talking about their apps.

Burak says

 A he wasn't surprised Azra won the competition.

 B he would like to use Azra's app.

 C it took Azra a long time to design her app.

> You have to answer a question or complete a sentence. Remember, only one of the three answers is correct.

**1** **Read the text again and match the sentence halves.**

1 The first app
2 If you want to download an app,
3 The most popular apps
4 Companies sometimes need a lot of money

a tell you about the news and the weather.
b if they want to make an app.
c was a game.
d you'll be able to choose from more than two million.

**2** **Read and complete the definition with words in the box.**

> application   download   laptop   program

**App** *noun* [c] the short word for an ¹_____ . A computer ²_____ or piece of software that you can ³_____ onto a cell phone or ⁴_____ .

**3** **Answer the questions to design your app.**

What will it do?

How will it look?

My App

What problem is it going to solve?

How will it make life easier?

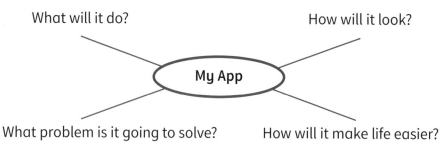

**4** **Draw a wireframe to show how your app will look.**

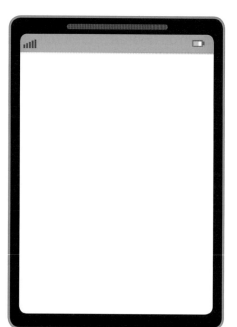

**1** **Answer the questions.**

What's your name?    Where do you live?

How old are you?

**2** **Answer the questions.**

Now let's talk about clothes. Where do you like shopping for clothes?

What kind of clothes do you like to buy?

Who helps you choose your clothes?

What clothes do you like to wear on weekends?

Now, please tell me something about clothing stores that are close to your house.

Now let's talk about technology. What do you do most when you use a cell phone?

Where do you use your laptop?

What new software would you like to buy?

Do you like to play video games?

Now, please tell me something about the technology you use in school.

| My progress: | | |
|---|---|---|
| I understood and answered all the questions. ☐ | I understood and answered most of the questions. ☐ | I didn't understand all the questions and needed some help. ☐ |

**1** **Read the text. Then choose the correct answer.**

## Using the Internet

### Alan

I have a laptop and it's usually in my bedroom. Sometimes my brother takes it to watch a movie and I can't find it. He can't understand why I get angry! I use the web to download games or find out how to repair my laptop. There's lots of useful help online, so I'm never worried. I don't like shopping for clothes online. It's not safe and you can't always get your money back.

### Greg

When I go out, I always take my phone. I usually ask, "What's the Wi-Fi password?" in cafés and friends' houses. I love looking for new clothes online and I need a fast connection! My parents check that I am using safe websites. You have to be careful and tell an adult if you are worried about what you should or shouldn't do online.

### Penny

For important homework, like research for geography, I always use my computer. I have my dad's old one. It's pretty slow, but that's OK! The best thing about the Internet is that you can find information about any school subject. The worst thing is that not everything you find is true. You have to check several web pages before you finish! But that takes time and I worry about feeling tired. If I don't finish by 11 p.m., I'll be tired the next day.

| | | Alan | Greg | Penny |
|---|---|---|---|---|
| 1 | Which person is interested in fashion? | A | B | C |
| 2 | Which person is worried about going to bed late? | A | B | C |
| 3 | Which person doesn't mind having a computer that isn't fast? | A | B | C |
| 4 | Which person has a family member who uses his/her computer? | A | B | C |
| 5 | Which person doesn't talk about a computer? | A | B | C |
| 6 | Which person has learned about computer software? | A | B | C |
| 7 | Which person talks about asking for help if you don't feel safe using the Internet? | A | B | C |

My progress: ____ /7

**②**

## 1 Complete the sentences with the first conditional.

1   If Alejandro drops his mom's cell phone in the bath, _____ .

2   If Ben and Tom wear the color blue to soccer practice, _____ .

3   If you don't eat breakfast before going to school, _____ .

## 2 Match the sentence halves.

1   If you put salt in Grandpa's coffee,

2   If we don't have Internet,

3   If we don't leave now,

4   If Sophie doesn't call when she gets home,

5   If it rains when we're at the beach,

6   If it's too hot,

a   we don't build sandcastles.

b   we'll be late.

c   her parents will be worried.

d   he won't be happy.

e   our cat sleeps under the bed.

f   we can't email.

## 3 Write one zero conditional sentence and one first conditional sentence that are true for you.

*I feel sad if I don't talk to my friends every day.*

*If I get a new laptop for my birthday, I'll be really happy.*

## 4 Complete the sentences with technology words.

1   A k _ y _ o _ r _ is h _ r _ w _ r _ that you use with a computer to write.

2   Now, left–c _ i _ k twice on the m _ u _ e and e _ t _ r the website.

3   You haven't spoken to your brother for a long time. Please t _ x _ or e _ a _ l him.

4   You can't d _ w _ l _ a _ anything because we don't have the Internet here.
    Here's a game on a d _ s _ . Put it in your l _ p _ o _ .

## 5 In pairs, answer the questions.

1   What is the most important technology you have at home?

> The most important technology I have at home is my cell phone. I can use it for lots of different things.

2   If you buy a computer in 2030, what will it be able to do?

> If I buy a computer in 2030, it will be able to do everything! I won't have to do my homework or turn off the lights or send my friends birthday cards.

# Review  •••  Units 1–2

**1  Match the sentence halves.**

| | | |
|---|---|---|
| 1 | The movie | **a** will leave without you! |
| 2 | If you're late, the bus | **b** weren't as expensive as I thought. |
| 3 | If you don't do your homework, I | **c** starts at 12:22 today. |
| 4 | The DVDs | **d** as quickly as possible. |
| 5 | He always does his homework | **e** 'll be upset. |

**2  Complete the sentences with the correct word.**

1  My sneakers aren't as old as my shoes. My shoes are _____ .

2  The computer store _____ at 9:00 tomorrow morning. It's open from 9:00 to 12:00 on Saturdays.

3  If you try on the sweater, I know you _____ love it!

4  If you _____ the pictures, everyone in your family can see them.

**3**  Underline the incorrect word. Then write the sentence correctly.

1  <u>When</u> Sam wears new clothes to my party, <u>I am</u> surprised.

If Sam wears new clothes to my party, I'll be surprised.

2  If you will click on the video link, you'll see Ronaldo score an amazing goal!

_____

3  This shirt isn't as big so that shirt.

_____

4  The movie is starts at 7 p.m.

_____

5  If I'm hungry, I'll eating something.

_____

**4  Complete the words in the sentences.**

1  I've lost my big blue wool s w e a t e r !

2  I can't d_____ the video on to my c_____ p_____ right now, because I don't have Wi-Fi.

3  My brother has to wear a shirt with a c_____ and bright blue t____ to school. It's his school uniform.

4  Oh, no! The s_____ on my l_____ is broken. I can't do my homework.

5  I'm trying to d_____ this album, but my Internet is very slow!

**1**   **Eliza's pen pal, Abigail, is coming for a week during summer vacation. Read Eliza's email.**

> ¹Hi Abigail!
>
> ²How are you? ³Can we go biking together when you're here in July? If we ride our bikes in the forest close to my house, we'll get very dirty, so you need to bring old clothes. Do you have a helmet? Your plane arrives at 12:20 and my dad can pick you up from the airport with his car.
>
> ⁴See you soon!
>
> Eliza

**2**   **Read Eliza's email again. Has Eliza ...**

- asked Abigail to go biking?
- said what clothes she needs to take?
- said how Abigail can contact her?
- given details of where they'll meet?

**3**   **Look at the green expressions in Eliza's email.** Here are some other expressions she could use. Circle the two best expressions in each line.

| 1 | Dear Miss Green | Hey, Abigail! | Hi, Abigail! |
|---|---|---|---|
| 2 | How's things? | I hope you are well. | How's tricks? |
| 3 | Do you feel like going ... ? | I would like to invite you to go ... | How about going ... ? |
| 4 | From, Eliza | Bye for now, Eliza | Best wishes, Eliza |

**4**   **Your American pen pal, Jane, is coming to your house for a week during the vacation.**

   **Write an email to Jane.**

In the email:

- **ask** Jane **to go swimming** with you
- say **what clothes** she needs to bring
- say **what time** you'll go to the airport

Write **25 words** or more.

# 3 Jim-nastics

## My goal

**Mission Complete!**

**5** I can communicate my opinion on a topic.

**4** I can write simple texts saying what I have done.

**3** I can say if sentences are true or not and give reasons.

**2** I can find certain information in a text.

 **1** I can solve a simple puzzle using pictures.

I can find certain information in a text.

### And I need ...

### To do this, I will ...

### So I can ...

### I want to practice ...

### ⦿ Diary

What I already know about sports ...

What I have learned about sports ...

**1** Look and write the words in the crossword.

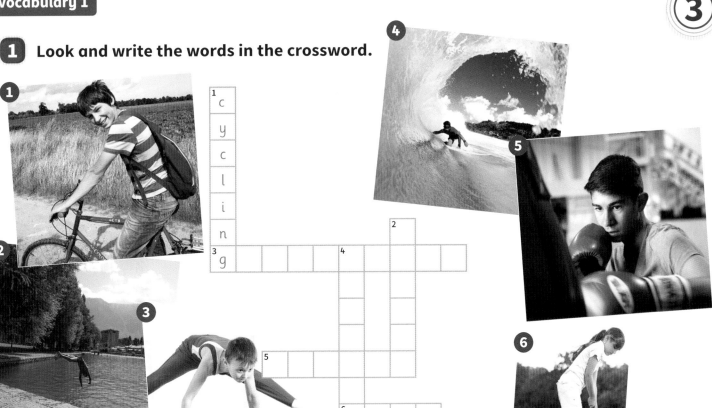

```
1 c
  y
  c
  l
  i
  n
3 g [ ][ ][ ][ ]  4 [ ][ ][ ]
                     [ ]
                     [ ]
                  5 [ ][ ][ ][ ]
                     [ ]
                  6 [ ][ ][ ][ ]
```

**2** Complete the sentences with the sports words.

1  My favorite sport is c_____t. It's a traditional sport in England and it's also popular in India and Australia.

2  Samuel plays r_____y in school. It's a very fast game with an unusual ball.

3  Do you like running, jumping, or throwing? Then you should try t_____k a__d f_____d!

4  I went w____r s_____g when I was in Spain last year. The sea was very cold!

5  I_e h_____y is a dangerous sport. It's very popular in the U.S.A. and Canada.

**3** In pairs, talk about popular sports in your country.

> Cycling is a very popular sport here. I know lots of people who cycle. My sister cycled 20 kilometers over the weekend.

**1** **Read the interview.** Which animal does James talk about?

## Talk to Tim

In my "Talk to Tim" column this week, I'm talking to James in 8th grade who has a very interesting hobby.

*Ooooh, that's an awesome picture, James. Where were you?*

I was in the south of France, but I wasn't on vacation. I was preparing for a competition.

*You're wearing diving equipment here. I didn't know there were diving competitions.*

Well, there are, but I was taking part in something much more exciting. Underwater cycling!

*But that's impossible! You can't cycle underwater.*

Oh, yes, you can. It isn't a very well-known sport, but you can do it in many places around the world – the U.S.A., Spain, England.

*What equipment do you need?*

As you can see in the picture, I have a tank on my back. This has my air to breathe. Then you need a wetsuit and mask for your eyes and face. And a bike of course.

*Is it a normal bike? One you can ride to school?*

Oh, no. It's heavy, very, very heavy. You have to cycle nearly a kilometer underwater and you can't put your feet on the ground.

*How many people take part?*

There are usually around ten people, and for every cyclist, there are two divers watching. If there's a problem, the divers get help.

*So, it isn't a dangerous sport.*

Not really. If you do it in the sea, the only real danger is the jellyfish! I think waterskiing and diving are more dangerous.

*And how did you do, James? Did you win?*

Not this time, no. But I came in fourth! My friends were very sad, but it was my first competition, so I'm very happy!

**2** **Look at the picture again and label the equipment.**

**3** ⭐ **Read the interview again and choose the correct answer.**

1 Underwater cycling is a sport that is

   **A** popular in the U.S.A.

   **B** only done in France.

   **C** practiced in many countries.

2 To do underwater cycling, you don't need

   **A** a digital camera.

   **B** a special bike.

   **C** something to cover your face.

3 The divers

   **A** take part in the competition.

   **B** watch the cyclists' feet.

   **C** help if something goes wrong.

4 What does James say about the competition?

   **A** He was sad that he lost.

   **B** He didn't come first this time.

   **C** He had more fun at other competitions.

## ⭐ Grammar: the passive (simple present)

**1** **Complete the sentences with the correct form of the words in parentheses.**

1  Diving __is watched__ by millions of people during the Olympic Games. (watch)

2  A small white ball _____ in golf. (use)

3  Rugby _____ in my school. (play)

4  _____ boxing _____ by anyone at your school? (practice)

5  Gymnastics and track and field _____ in American schools. (teach)

6  Many sports _____ on television. (show)

**2** **Order the words to make sentences.**

1  every year in / 3 million / are / bikes / sold / More than / the U.K.

_____

2  served / is / rice. / Chinese / with / food

_____

3  Japanese / in your school? / Is / by / spoken / many people

_____

4  isn't / in a / Ice hockey / played / swimming pool.

_____

5  used / Tablets / aren't / in tests. / and phones

_____

**3** **Read the example and write silly sentences.** Use the words to help you.

octopus   whale   actor   spaceship   school

butterfly   restaurant   snowman   astronaut

uniform   sunglasses   tights   gloves

laptop   noodles   bandages   car   plane

make   drive   wear   sell   buy   eat   fly

Oliver the Octopus had an accident. His arms are covered in bandages and he can't use his laptop!

_____

**1** **Look and complete the conversations.**

**1**

**Clara:** That's an awesome picture. Who is it?

**Laura:** It's Misael Rodríguez. He won a bronze medal in the 2016 Olympics.

**Clara:** Great, but why isn't he wearing a ___helmet___?

**Laura:** Boxers don't wear them. I don't know why – it's a very dangerous sport!

**2**

**Pedro:** That's Alberto Contador, isn't it?

**Diego:** Yes, this is him.

**Pedro:** He's my favorite _____.

**3**

**Chen:** Wow – great picture!

**Jasmine:** Thanks! I took it when I went to London.

**Chen:** What is it?

**Jasmine:** It's a track and field _____! It's the highest in London.

**4**

**Matt:** This is Alison Teal close to the river Seine in Paris.

**Helen:** What's she doing?

**Matt:** She thinks our rivers and seas are too dirty.

**Helen:** So she surfs in dirty water?

**Matt:** Yes. She always wears pink and has a pink _____. Then when pictures of her are in newspapers …

**Helen:** People learn more about the problem.

**5**

**Emma:** Everybody knows who they are. Ronaldo and …

**Joanna:** Ramos. The best players in the best team in the world Real Madrid.

**Emma:** No, it's Barcelona for me. Remember Messi in 2012? He scored the most _____.

**6**

**Leila:** Where's that?

**Mira:** Nanjing in China. It's a school for young gymnasts.

**Leila:** They're very young.

**Mira:** Yes, and they _____ every day.

**2** **Write two questions about Activity 1. Ask and answer in pairs.**

1 _____    2 _____

**3** 🎧 5.07 **Listen and complete Emma's diary with one word in each blank.**

Zoe (my tennis [1]_____) called.

I have to meet her and Leah (new girl) tomorrow at 4 p.m. on [2]_____ 2.

BUT can Leah [3]_____ the ball? Or does it go in the [4]_____?

I HAVE TO take my [5]_____!

## ★ Grammar: modal verbs

**1** **Choose the correct answer.**

1 I (might) / can get 100,000 views for my gymnastics blog, but I'm not sure.

2 James **may not** / **should** have been riding his bike today – his bike broke last night.

3 We **will** / **could** go to the Indian restaurant tonight if you like. It's your choice.

4 **Might** / **Can** we meet at Lisa's house after school? Her house is close to the park.

5 **Might not** / **Can** we watch the game later? Messi's going to play, and he's my favorite soccer player!

6 We **will** / **might not** win the game – we're the best players and we've scored ten goals!

**2** **Complete the sentences with the words in the box.**

| can | might | can | will |
| --- | --- | --- | --- |

1 Nadal has won more games than Murray. I'm sure Nadal _____ win the game.

2 Emily knows how to skate and hit a ball at the same time! She _____ like ice skating.

3 I like eating paella. _____ we go to Manuel's on the weekend?

4 We _____ see Iker Casillas play tomorrow, but we have to wait until the coach decides.

## Speaking

**3**  **Watch Pablo and Ezgi doing some speaking practice.**

**4**  **Watch again.** **Complete the sentences with the words in the box.**

| also | Because | like |
| --- | --- | --- |

**Teacher:** Now, do you prefer playing team sports or individual sports, Pablo?

**Pablo:** Um, team sports, I think.

**Teacher:** Why?

**Pablo:** ¹_____ it's more fun!

**Pablo:** I play soccer and I'm ²_____ on my town's basketball team.

**Ezgi:** I prefer individual sports, ³_____ track and field.

> **SPEAKING TIP!** Answer the questions fully. Think of reasons, examples, and extra things to say.

> **PRONUNCIATION TIP!** Use contractions when you speak because they are less formal.

**5** 📝 **Now plan your answers to the questions. Use the words in Activity 4.**

**1 Read the story again.** Connect the pictures in the correct order and number the pictures.

**2 Read and answer the questions.**

**Cynisca's fact sheet**

1 Where did she live? _____ in Ancient Greece _____
2 Who was her father? _____
3 Who was her brother? _____
4 Which sport did she love? _____
5 When did she first win the Olympics? _____
6 What did she win it for? _____

**3 Read the example.** Then write about something you worked hard to achieve.

I wanted a higher score on my math test. I practiced with my friend who is good at math and
I studied ten minutes extra every day. _____

_____

_____

**4** Look and guess which sports were in the Olympic Games in Ancient Greece.

**5** ⭐ Read the text and choose the correct answer.

In 776 B.C.E., about three thousand years ago, the first Olympic Games took place in Olympia, Greece. It was a festival for Zeus, a Greek god and they celebrated it every four years. Only men and boys could go to see the games. Girls and women could not go into the stadium. The athletes had to be free men, not slaves, and they had to speak Greek.

Up to 50,000 people could sit in the stadium. It was hot and there wasn't much water, but lots of people still went to watch. There were all kinds of acrobats and fun things to see. The Games ended with a giant barbecue.

There were many popular events at the ancient Olympics, such as running, throwing, the long jump, horse racing, and chariot races. However, the Pankration was the nastiest one. It was a lot like boxing, and men did anything to win. They hit the other players or threw sand in their eyes. However, breaking the rules was very bad.

The Olympics were so important to the Greeks that all enemies stopped fighting battles with each other for a month before the games started. During this time, athletes trained for the events and they could travel to the games safely.

The Ancient Olympic Games stopped in 393 C.E. The Modern Olympic Games that we know today didn't start again until 1896, almost 1500 years later.

**1** What is the best title for the article?
   A The Ancient Olympic Games
   B The Pankration
   C Ancient Olympic Stadiums

**2** Who couldn't go to the games?
   A men
   B young boys and girls
   C girls and women

**3** Athletes in the Ancient Olympic Games
   A were slaves.
   B wore special clothes.
   C had to speak Greek.

**4** The Olympic stadium
   A was very big.
   B had a river nearby.
   C didn't have space for lots of people.

**1** **Read the quiz and choose the best answers for you.**

# How healthy are you?

**1** How much exercise do you do a day?
  **A** 0–30 minutes
  **B** 30–60 minutes
  **C** 60 minutes or more

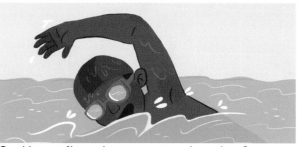

**3** How often do you go swimming?
  **A** never
  **B** only in the summer
  **C** once a week

**2** How often do you walk/ride a bike to school?
  **A** never
  **B** one or two times a week
  **C** more than two times a week

**4** How much time do you spend watching TV or playing video games?
  **A** more than two hours
  **B** one to two hours
  **C** no more than one hour

**Mostly As:** You should try to do 30 minutes of exercise a few times a week. Could you walk to school or go to the park and play soccer with your friends?

**Mostly Bs:** You are doing well, but perhaps you could think about riding your bike to school more often and watching a bit less TV.

**Mostly Cs:** Excellent! You have an active life

**2** **In pairs, think of ways to be more active.**

> I want to watch less television and swim once a week.

**1** 🎧 5.08 **For each question, write the correct answer in each blank.** Write **one word** or **a number** or **a date** or **a time**. You will hear a woman talking about a new sports center.

### NEW SPORTS CENTER

**Name of Sports Center:**    Murray

**Address:**    1 _____ Road

**Opened on:**    2 _____ 6th

**Soccer field:**    in the 3 _____

**Team sports:**    volleyball and 4 _____

**For more information, call:**    5 _____

**1** **For these questions, write the correct answer in each blank.**
**Write ONE word for each blank.**

---

From: Neil                    To: Jess

Hi!

I want to tell you about my new rugby club. Yesterday we studied the history
¹ _____ the sport. My coach said that people played rugby in ² _____
19th century, but it only became really popular in the 20th century.

³ _____ you know that the first U.K. women's rugby team started in 1962? Another
surprise was that the special ball was between 410 and 460 grams. I also learned that
⁴ _____ longest game ever was more than 26 hours long. Just think how tired the
players were!

I have ⁵ _____ new boots to show you, but they're ⁶ _____ very comfortable!

See you soon,

Neil

---

**1 Complete the sentences with the correct form of the verbs in parentheses.**

1 Surfboards ___are made___ of wood. (make)

2 A ball _____ in ice hockey. (not/use)

3 Soccer and basketball _____ in many countries. (play)

4 Helmets _____ by cyclists. (wear)

5 Surfing _____ in towns by the sea. (do)

6 Cricket _____ in schools in England. (teach)

**2 Complete the sentences with the verbs in the box.**

> Can   can   could   might   will

1 Sophie _____ buy a new racket today, but she isn't sure.

2 _____ we go surfing today? The weather's good.

3 James _____ play golf very well. He can hit the ball a long way.

4 We _____ watch Madrid play Barcelona later, if you like.

5 I _____ see you on court 3 at 2 p.m., I promise.

**3 Write two sentences with modal verbs that are true for you.**

> I can play basketball very well.

> I might visit my grandparents today.

_____

_____

**4 Complete the sentences with the sports words.**

1 You have to have a s_____ to go s_____ .

2 My t___ k___ n___ i___ l___ coach is very nice. She teaches me to run fast.

3 It's important to wear a h_____ if you do b_____ .

4 You hit the puck into the g_____ in i____ h_____ .

5 Don't forget your r_____ if you want to play tennis today.

**5 In pairs, answer the questions.**

1 What's your favorite sport now? And your least favorite? Why?

2 Which sport might you try in the future? Why?

> Well, my least favorite sport is swimming because I HATE cold water!

# 4 Be careful!

## My goal

I can give advice to my friends. **5**

**Mission Complete!**

I can give personal details about my age and where I live. **4**

**3** I can write an answer to an email.

I can understand a code and use it to complete a conversation. **2**

I can understand common words about illnesses. **1**

### And I need ...

### To do this, I will ...

### So I can ...

### I want to practice ...

## Diary

What I already know about being careful ...

What I have learned about being careful ...

**1** Order the letters and write the words.

| c e y e r g m e n e   r o d o | e n t p t i a | a r h e t | n f p u a l i |
|---|---|---|---|
| | patient | | |

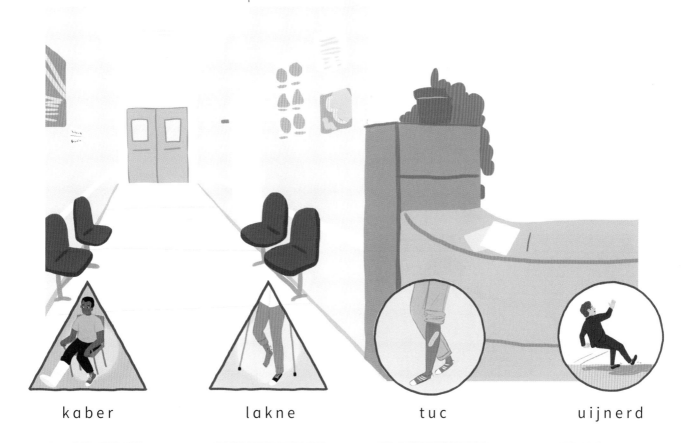

| k a b e r | l a k n e | t u c | u i j n e r d |
|---|---|---|---|

**2** Use the words in the signs to make sentences.

Quick, quick! There's an emergency here! My friend has broken his ankle.

**3** In pairs, say three sentences with the words in the signs. Your partner guesses if they are true.

I fell off my bike last year and broke my leg.

No, you didn't! You don't have a bike!

**1** Write sentences with *might*, *may*, or *could* and the words in the box.

Be careful!    Look out!    Watch out!

**2** 5.09 **Listen and order the pictures.**

**3** 5.10 ⭐ **Listen. For each question, choose the correct answer.**

1   You will hear two people talking on the phone. Who is Rosie?

    **A**   a vet
    **B**   a doctor
    **C**   a pet

2   You will hear two people talking about a little boy. Where is the little boy?

    **A**   in a café
    **B**   in an ambulance
    **C**   outside a hospital

3   You will hear two boys talking about an accident. What was Martin doing when it happened?

    **A**   playing rugby
    **B**   playing a video game
    **C**   getting out of bed

4   You will hear a news anchor talking about an accident. Where did it happen?

    **A**   in a kitchen
    **B**   in a restaurant
    **C**   in a hotel

## ★ Grammar: the present perfect

**1** **Complete the sentences with the words in parentheses.**

1 He isn't in school because he 's injured _____ his ankle. (injure)

2 We _____ the doctor since this morning. (see)

3 I can't play soccer because I _____ my leg. (break)

4 _____ Noa _____ her friend in the hospital? (visit)

5 Catalina _____ a bandage on her arm for a week. (have)

6 How long _____ you _____ a patient in this hospital? (be)

**2** **Order the words to make sentences.**

1 since / I / you / five. / haven't / you / seen / were

_____

2 the / How / car? / in / have / long / been / we

_____

3 He / since / hasn't / breakfast. / eaten

_____

4 lived / three / They / years. / Sydney / have / for / in

_____

**3** ★ **Read and complete the text.**

| Wall | Find friends | Chat | | Profile | Sign out |

Hi Benjamin,

How are you? I've been in my new school here in Datong now ¹___for___ three weeks! I ² _____ made lots of new friends and I've joined the soccer team. ⚽ I injured my leg last week, but I'm OK now.

I sit next to a boy named Fai. He loves reading and he ³ _____ read most of the books in the library! 📖 ⁴ _____ you read the one about the evil dentist? It's our favorite.

How are your brothers? I ⁵ _____ seen them ⁶ _____ your birthday party. See you all in Barcelona next summer. 🎆

Message me soon,

Wang

**4** **You're Benjamin. Reply to Wang and tell him what you've done since you last saw him.**

Hi, Wang! Thanks for writing! Your school sounds great. Since I last saw you, I …

_____

**1** **Look at the code and complete the conversations.**

| A | B | C | D | E | F | G | H | I | J | K | L | M |
|---|---|---|---|---|---|---|---|---|---|---|---|---|
| ⇨ | ⇨ | ⇨ | ⇨ | ⇨ | ← | → | ↑ | ↓ | ↖ | ↗ | ↙ | ↘ |
| **N** | **O** | **P** | **Q** | **R** | **S** | **T** | **U** | **V** | **W** | **X** | **Y** | **Z** |
| ↔ | ↕ | ▲ | ▼ | △ | ▽ | ◀ | ▶ | ◁ | ▷ | ◤ | ◢ | ◸ |

**1** Grace: Emma's having an ↕▲⇨△⇨◀↓↕↔ ___operation___ on her back today.

Mandy: Ouch. Poor Emma!

**2** Matt: What's the matter with your foot?

Maria: I dropped my school bag on it. Look at my ⇨⇨↔⇨→⇨ _____ – it's enormous!

Matt: Oooops! ↙↓⇨ _____ ⇨↕▷↔ _____ and △⇨▽◀ _____ .

**3** Dr. Jones: Hi, Mrs. Greene. What's the matter today?

Mrs. Greene: I think I have the ←↙▶ _____ . I feel terrible, I feel sick, I have a headache …

Dr. Jones: OK. Here's a ▲△⇨▽⇨△↓▲◀↓↕↔ _____ for some medicine. Take one ▲↓↙↙ _____ twice a day. I hope you ←⇨⇨↙ _____ ⇨→◀⇨△ _____ soon.

Mrs. Greene: Thanks, Doctor.

**2** **Look and complete the text.**

This is a picture of my sister, Lucy. She has the [1] _ l _ . She has to [2] _ i _ _ _ _ w _ and [3] _ e _ _ _ . Dad has given her some [4] _ e _ _ _ _ i _ _ _ . I hope she [5] _ e _ _ _ e _ _ _ r soon.

**3** **Your friends need your advice. Tell them what to do.**

**1** I fell over when I was running upstairs. I've hurt my ankle.

Sit down for a few minutes. You should be careful when you're running upstairs!

**2** I haven't felt well for a week. My head, my throat, my ears … everything hurts!

**3** I'm really, really tired. I was reading my favorite book last night and I didn't finish until midnight!

## ★ Grammar: the present progressive for future plans

**1** **Complete the sentences with the words in parentheses.**

1 My mom's in the hospital, so I 'm taking ___ her some flowers and chocolate later. (take)

2 Cara has a painful leg, so she ___ dancing tonight. (not go)

3 ___ they ___ their grandmother this evening? (visit)

4 ___ she ___ in the ocean with a bandage on her foot after lunch? (swim)

5 Fred ___ some medicine for his cough from the drugstore this afternoon. (buy)

6 ___ we ___ to Rome or going by train? (fly)

## Speaking

**2**  **Watch Pablo and Ezgi doing some speaking practice. Answer the questions.**

1 Who talks about illnesses? ___

2 Who talks about accidents? ___

> **SPEAKING TIP!** You don't have to tell the truth! If you can't think of an example, you can invent one.

**3** ▶ **Watch again. Answer the questions.**

1 How old was Pablo when he had his accident?

___

2 How long was Ezgi in the hospital?

___

3 Who gives the most information?

___

4 Who do you think is telling the truth? Why?

___

**4** **Now plan your answers to the questions.**

___

___

___

___

**5** ▶ **Watch the video again. Listen and underline the stressed words in these questions.**

1 Ezgi, how old are you?

2 Where do you live?

3 Did you go to the hospital?

> **PRONUNCIATION TIP!** Try to use the correct sentence stress. People will understand you better.

**1** **Read the story and answer the questions.**

1 Why is Chloe excited about the local news program?

_____

2 Who are the two men under the tree?

_____

3 When does Joshua hurt himself?

_____

4 Why doesn't Joshua follow his cousin and sister over the bridge?

_____

5 Why doesn't Joshua jump into the river?

_____

**2** **Read and write the words in the crossword.**

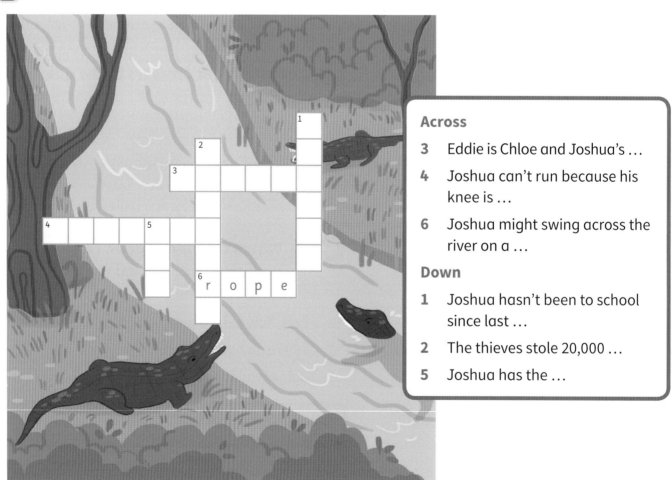

**Across**

3 Eddie is Chloe and Joshua's …

4 Joshua can't run because his knee is …

6 Joshua might swing across the river on a …

**Down**

1 Joshua hasn't been to school since last …

2 The thieves stole 20,000 …

5 Joshua has the …

**3** **Joshua has fallen asleep again.** Choose what happens in the second part of his dream and write about it.

He's hurt his knee

Ask his friends to help him

**Problems Joshua has**

**Things Joshua can do**

**What happens in the end**

His friends carry him away

**4** ★ **Look at the pictures.** In pairs, answer the questions.

Do you like these different activities? Why?

Which of these activities do you like best? Why?

Do you think watching television is fun?

Do you think climbing trees is dangerous?

Do you think making your own necklaces is boring?

Do you think learning about animals is important?

**1** 🎧 5.11 ⭐ **Listen and complete the chart about a famous scientist.**

**Name:** Marie Curie

**Date of birth:** [1]_____ 1867

**Place of birth:** [2]_____, Poland

**University:** Sorbonne, [3]_____

**Subject at university:** [4]_____

**Discovered:** Polonium and [5]_____

**Prizes:** 1903 Nobel Prize in [6]_____ and 1911 Nobel Prize in [7]_____

**Died:** July 4th [8]_____

**2** **Write about an important scientist or doctor from your country.**

**Name:** _____
**Date of birth:** _____
**Place of birth:** _____
**University:** _____
**What they studied:** _____
**Why they are important:** _____
_____
**Prizes:** _____
**Died:** _____
**How they have changed our lives:** _____
_____
_____

**1** For these questions, choose the correct answer for each blank.

**Wilhelm C Röntgen**

After a game like soccer, a person might get an X-ray if they ¹_____ their leg or arm. An X-ray shows if something is broken, and it also shows other ²_____ of the body, like the heart. A dentist can use X-rays to look at teeth, and airport workers use an X-ray machine to check suitcases or laptops before a ³_____ leaves.

In 1895, Wilhelm Röntgen found out about X-rays by accident. He was studying electricity when he ⁴_____ an idea. He took an X-ray picture of his wife's hand, and saw the fingers on ⁵_____ hand and the ring which she was wearing. The "x" in the word X-ray is there because Wilhelm couldn't explain exactly how it worked. He just knew that X-rays were new and useful for science.

He won a prize and a lot of money in 1901, but he gave it all to his college. He died in 1923 in Germany. Today you can visit a ⁶_____ about Röntgen's life in the city where he was born.

| | | | | | | |
|---|---|---|---|---|---|---|
| **1** | **A** | hurt | **B** | pain | **C** | sore |
| **2** | **A** | things | **B** | places | **C** | parts |
| **3** | **A** | taxi | **B** | train | **C** | plane |
| **4** | **A** | made | **B** | had | **C** | did |
| **5** | **A** | the | **B** | her | **C** | hers |
| **6** | **A** | museum | **B** | hotel | **C** | movie theater |

My progress: [ ] /6

**1**  **5.12** **Listen. For each question, choose the correct answer.**

1 You hear a nurse talking in a hospital. What does he say about his job right now?

    **A** It's pretty difficult.

    **B** He's in a smaller hospital now.

    **C** He sometimes forgets to give medicine.

2 You hear two friends talking about a movie on TV. What did the girl enjoy most?

    **A** the actor

    **B** the music

    **C** the moon

3 You hear part of a program about playing basketball. What is the most important thing?

    **A** buying basketballs

    **B** choosing where to play

    **C** practicing with a friend

4 You hear a girl talking on the phone. What's the matter?

    **A** She has a headache.

    **B** She's hungry.

    **C** She hit her head on the sofa.

5 You hear a teacher talking about a classroom. What does he want to know?

    **A** Why the printer is on his desk.

    **B** Who closed the window.

    **C** Who was playing soccer.

**My progress:** ☐ /5

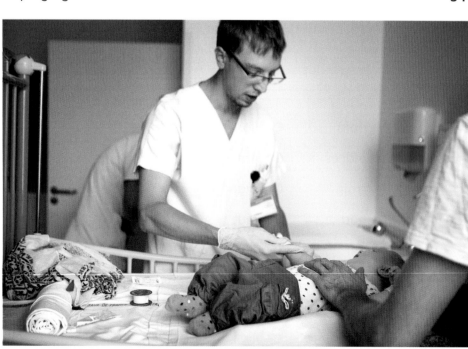

## 1 Complete the sentences with the words in parentheses and *how long*, *for*, or *since*.

1  I _____haven't watched_____ TV _____since_____ last month. (not watch)

2  Maite _____ on her ankle _____ a week. (not walk)

3  They _____ at Disneyland _____ Monday. (be)

4  _____ Ben _____ a painful arm? (have)

5  We _____ in bed with the flu _____ two days. (be)

6  Kim isn't here. She _____ to the doctor's. (go)

## 2 Complete the conversation with the words in the box.

> buy   come   get   ~~go~~   take   wear

**Naomi:** ¹ _____Are_____ you _____going_____ to Sophie's party tomorrow?

**Kelly:** Yes, I am. What ² _____ you _____?

**Naomi:** Well, I have a new dress. How ³ _____ you _____ there?

**Kelly:** Kevin's mom ⁴ _____ me. Come with us! They ⁵ _____ to my house at 3 p.m.

**Naomi:** Perfect. Have you bought her a present?

**Kelly:** No, I haven't. I'm ⁶ _____ her clothes this year. I think a T-shirt is a good idea.

**Naomi:** Great! See you tomorrow!

## 3 Write one thing that you have or haven't done today and one thing you are doing later today.

_____

_____

## 4 Match the sentence halves.

1  I'm really tired today. I'm          a  feel better soon.

2  She's having an                      b  the doctor, Mrs. Brown?

3  I hope you                           c  headache for two days.

4  I've had a bad                       d  resting at home and watching TV this evening.

5  Are you here to see                  e  operation on her toe today.

## 5 Continue the conversation in pairs.

What are you doing after school today?

I'm going straight to the library to do my homework, then I'm …

# Review ••• Units 3–4

## 1 Complete the sentences with the correct word.

1 Helmets _are_____ usually worn by cyclists at the Olympic Games.

2 I _____ have read the schedule wrong.

3 _____ we go to soccer practice?

4 I'm not _____ to the movies tomorrow night.

5 She's _____ feeling sick since this morning.

6 This cake was _____ by my mom.

## 2 Underline the incorrect word. Then write the sentence correctly.

1 Lucia has the flu since Monday.
   _Lucia has had the flu since Monday._____

2 A point scored when the player shoots the basketball in the net.
   _____

3 Felipe is teach by his coach, Roberto.
   _____

4 May he play tennis well?
   _____

5 It can rain tonight, so remember to bring your raincoat.
   _____

6 I cook fish tonight.
   _____

## 3 Complete the words in the sentences.

1 Feng does _track_____ and field every Wednesday. He wears a red s_____ with his club's name.

2 Ignacio! You don't have your r_____, and you're on the wrong tennis c_____!

3 I always wear my h_____ when I ride my bike.

4 Who is your dad's favorite s_____ player?

5 Do i___ h_____ players feel cold when they're playing?

## 4 Complete the sentences.

1 How long have you _been_____ living in the rain forest?

2 I _____ eating in a famous restaurant next week.

3 Are you _____ the soccer game on TV tonight?

4 He's been on vacation _____ the beginning of the month.

5 We haven't seen Mike _____ three days.

**1** Read Luisa's blog about how she stays safe doing school sports. Answer the questions.

**Luisa's Sports Blog**

Here are three ways to stay safe during school athletics. First, you should do your training the way your coach tells you. It might not be easy at first, but it keeps you safer. Next, warm-up so you can play without injuries. Last, use the right equipment. Here's me in my batting helmet, so I don't get hurt if the ball is thrown wrong. Have fun and stay safe!

1  What is the blog about? _____

2  What is Luisa's first way to stay safe? _____

3  Why should you warm up? _____

4  What sport does Luisa play? _____

5  Why does Luisa wear a batting helmet? _____

**2** Write notes about how to stay safe while doing fun summer activities.

Write one safety idea for each dangerous item. What should you do? Why?

| Sun/Heat | Water (pool, lake, ocean) | Injuries |
|---|---|---|
|  |  |  |

**3** Use your notes to write a blog about staying safe during summer fun. Write 30 words or more. Be sure to say what to do and why it will help.

_____

_____

_____

_____

_____

_____

_____

# 5 Fun foods

## My goal

I can look at information on a chart and explain why things happen. **5**

## Mission Complete!

I can express my opinion and give reasons for it. **3**

**4** I can describe a character's feelings.

I can write about a restaurant. **2**

I can read the names of foods in a café.

### And I need …

### To do this, I will …

### So I can …

### I want to practice …

## ⊚ Diary

What I already know about foods …

What I have learned about foods …

**1** **In pairs, talk about the pictures and guess the food.**

> What do you think picture 1 is?

> I don't know. It might be a mushroom.

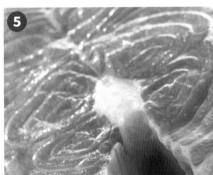
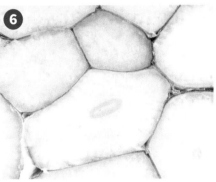

**2** **Order the letters and complete the food labels.**

## Salad Niçoise

**INGREDIENTS**

French green beans, lettuce, red potatoes, **easkt** _____, eggs, tomatoes, olives, **oli** _____, vinegar, parsley, thyme, **icgrla** _____, salt, pepper

Keep refrigerated.

Best before 10.2018

## Karima's Curry

**INGREDIENTS**

balm, chickpeas, tomatoes, spinach, coconut milk, onions, garlic, olive oil, **srbhe** _____ (turmeric, cilantro), curry leaves, ginger, curry powder, **lichi** _____ powder

Best before 11.2018

**3** **In pairs, choose three food items and say how often you eat them.**

> I never eat broccoli. I don't like it. I love cabbage and I eat it every week.

**1** ⭐ **Read the text and choose the correct answer.**

I went to the Rainforest Café in New York for my birthday last weekend with my parents and three friends from school. It's great for kids and adults and the ¹_____ is delicious. I had a ²_____ burger with fries, Lucy and Jessica had vegetarian pasta with cheese, broccoli, and lots of ³_____ , and Catarina chose ⁴_____ with potatoes. She loves fish. Mom and Dad had a good time, too. Dad had lamb with lots of vegetables and Mom ate chicken wings. We shared some ⁵_____ bread, salad, and onion rings. The fruit juices were awesome, too.

But the best part about the restaurant was the decoration! It was like a jungle with flowers, ⁶_____ , and big leaves everywhere. And there were jungle animals, too. They weren't real, of course (It's in New York, not Africa!), but there were lizards, ⁷_____ , and snakes by our table. At the end of the meal, we had a birthday ⁸_____ with lots of chocolate on top. I can't wait to go next year!

| | | | | | | | | | |
|---|---|---|---|---|---|---|---|---|---|
| **1** | **A** food | **B** music | **C** dancing | | **5** | **A** garlic | **B** broccoli | **C** cabbage |
| **2** | **A** onion | **B** oil | **C** steak | | **6** | **A** chairs | **B** drinks | **C** trees |
| **3** | **A** mushroom | **B** lamb | **C** herbs | | **7** | **A** dogs | **B** cats | **C** monkeys |
| **4** | **A** steak | **B** salmon | **C** lamb | | **8** | **A** song | **B** cake | **C** cookie |

**2** **Imagine this is your favorite restaurant.** Why do you like it? Write 25 words or more.

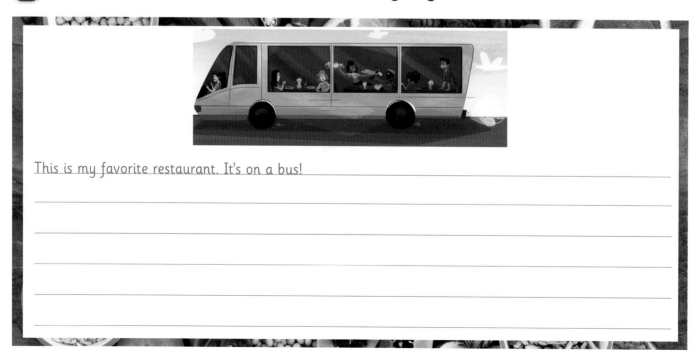

This is my favorite restaurant. It's on a bus! _____

_____

_____

_____

_____

## Grammar: *rather* and *prefer*

**1** **Complete the sentences with *prefer* or *rather*.**

1 Would you ___rather___ eat in a cafeteria or in a restaurant?

2 I _____ salmon to lamb, but I like all food!

3 I'd _____ not to have spicy food, thanks.

4 Would Dad _____ to have broccoli or cabbage with his steak?

5 Thiago would _____ to go to a café with Samantha.

6 She'd _____ see her friends for lunch.

**2** **Find the mistakes and write the sentences correctly.**

1 Would your cat rather to eat salmon or steak? ___Would your cat prefer to eat salmon or steak?___

2 Kieron and Caleb would not rather play chess. _____

3 We rather sit outside than inside. _____

4 Maria would prefer having a dog than a baby sister! _____

5 Juan would prefer not go to school today. _____

6 Would James preferring to play basketball or soccer? _____

**3** **Write questions about each pair of pictures using *rather* or *prefer*.**

1 **A**

2 **A**

3 **A**

**B**

**B**

**B**

Would you _____
_____ ?

**4**  **Listen and check the correct picture.** Did you ask the same questions?

**1** Order the letters and write the cooking words.

1 aepsucna _saucepan_     5 elttek _____     9 ceslid _____

2 utc _____     6 gfinry anp _____

3 yfr _____     7 arotrsc _____

4 hdsi _____     8 ledboi _____

**2** Choose words from Activity 1 and write possible and impossible sentences. Can your partner guess the impossible sentences?

I eat cereal from a frying pan.

I can boil water in a kettle.

_____

_____

_____

_____

**3** 🎧 5.14 Listen and choose the correct answer.

1 How old is Asli?

  A 8–13

  B 6–13

  C 8–18

2 The person who invented Asli's cake was

  A her grandmother.

  B her mother.

  C Asli.

3 The butter is in the

  A bowl.

  B frying pan.

  C dish.

4 The main ingredient in the cake is

  A salad.

  B a vegetable.

  C soup.

5 The cake takes

  A 14 minutes to cook.

  B 40 minutes to cook.

  C an hour and 40 minutes to cook.

## ★ Grammar: the passive (simple past)

**1 Complete the sentences and questions with the correct form of *be*.**

1 This steak is horrible. It _____was_____ fried for too long by the chef. ✓
2 _____ you told about the broccoli ice cream? ✓
3 Tammy and Sidney _____ invited to the party. ✗
4 The carrots _____ boiled for ten minutes. ✓
5 The jello _____ eaten at school. ✗
6 _____ he given a prize at the cooking competition? ✓

**2 Complete the text.**

First, water ¹ _____was put_____ in the saucepan. Then two eggs
² _____ (place) in the water. The water ³ _____ (boil) for
two minutes. The eggs ⁴ _____ (remove) and the tops of the eggs
⁵ _____ (cut off). The eggs ⁶ _____ (eat) with bread "soldiers"
– sliced toast. Boiled eggs and soldiers – yum!

## Speaking

**3 Watch Ezgi and Pablo doing some speaking practice.** Answer the questions.

1 Who is a vegetarian? _____
2 Who likes spicy food? _____

**4 Watch again. Who says each sentence and question? Write P (Pablo), E (Ezgi), or TE (Teacher).**

1 What do you think? ☐
2 I agree. ☐
3 Me, too. ☐
4 You're right. ☐
5 What do you think of school dinners? ☐
6 That's true. ☐
7 Which of these meals and restaurants do you like the best? ☐

**5 Now plan your answers to the questions.**

**SPEAKING TIP!** Try to give your own opinion and ask the other student what they think, too. Give reasons for your opinion.

**6 Watch the video again and listen. What word is used to emphasize how much they like something?**

**PRONUNCIATION TIP!** In "Yes/No" questions, the voice goes up at the end of the questions. In "Wh" questions, the voice goes down on the last stressed syllable of the question.

**1** **Answer the questions about** *The Very, Very Interesting Journal of Juana Sánchez.*

1 What do Carlos's parents think of the show?

2 What does he do on the show?

3 Why hasn't Juana watched the show?

4 Why does Juana put worms in Carlos's cooking pot?

**2** **Read the sentences.** Do you agree with them? Why/Why not? In pairs, discuss your ideas.

1 Carlos talks about his YouTube show too much.

> I agree. He should talk less about his show and let other people tell him what they think of it.

2 Carlos's parents should be as interested in Juana as they are in Carlos.

> I agree. Parents should talk to each of their children and be interested in them.

3 Carlos is horrible to Juana.

> I disagree. Carlos talks about himself a lot, but he isn't horrible to Juana.

4 Juana is horrible to Carlos.

> I agree. She puts worms in his pot, and that wasn't a very nice thing to do.

**3** **What do you think happens next?** Read the ideas and talk to your partner about them. Think of one idea of your own.

1 Carlos cooks something for Juana, but puts something horrible in it.

2 Juana tells Carlos she is very sorry, and says she will help him with his next show.

3 Juana's parents say they are very angry with her, and tell her that she can't go to the park with her friends over the weekend.

> I think Juana says sorry to Carlos, Carlos says "OK", and then Juana says she will help Carlos with his new videos.

**4** **Cooking is very important to Carlos.** Writing a journal is very important to Juana. What activities are important to you and why?

*Playing the guitar is very important to me. It helps me relax after school.*

**5** ⭐ **Read the two conversations below.** Which answer do you prefer and why?

**CONVERSATION 1**

**Teacher:** Good morning. What's your name?

**Student:** Javi.

**Teacher:** And where do you live?

**Student:** Madrid.

**Teacher:** OK. And how old are you, Javi?

**Student:** 11.

**CONVERSATION 2**

**Teacher:** Good morning. What's your name?

**Student:** Good morning. My name is Juana.

**Teacher:** And where do you live?

**Student:** I live in Monterrey. Close to the famous mountain called Cerro de Silla.

**Teacher:** OK. And how old are you, Juana?

**Student:** I'm ten years old. I'll be 11 in October.

**6** **In pairs, ask and answer the questions.**

1 Fact-based questions

   **A** What's your name?     **B** Where do you live?     **C** How old are you?

2 Topic-based questions

   **A** What's your favorite food?

   **B** What do you usually eat for breakfast?

   **C** Tell me something about the meals you eat with your family.

Speak in full sentences, e.g., say *I live in Madrid* not *Madrid* in answer to the question *Where do you live?*

**1** **Read the report below and answer the questions.** Then explain the results.

1    Which foods contain carbohydrates? _____

2    Which foods don't contain carbohydrates? _____

3    Which surprises you? _____

The results show _____ .

## Investigation to find carbohydrates in food

Iodine is a yellowish-brown liquid. When it comes into contact with carbohydrates, it turns dark blue or black.

| Food | Result |
|------|--------|
| Apple | yellow |
| Cooked rice | black |
| Cookie | dark blue |
| Carrot | yellow |
| Potato | dark blue |
| Pasta | black |
| Bread | black |

**2** 🎧 5.15 **Listen and complete the recipe.**

### Green super smoothie

INGREDIENTS

☐ One small [1]_____

☐ Half an avocado

☐ Two [2]_____ beans

☐ One cup of spinach leaves

☐ One cup of coconut [3]_____

☐ One tablespoon of
   [4]_____ juice.

**3** **Write the ingredients for your own smoothie.**

**Ingredients**

_____

_____

_____

_____

_____

_____

**1** 🎧 5.16 **Listen.** For each question, choose the correct answer. You will hear Johnny talking to his grandma about a school picture. When did he meet these people?

| People | | Month | |
|---|---|---|---|
| **1** Michel | ☐ | **A** May | |
| **2** Tom | ☐ | **B** September | |
| **3** Susie | ☐ | **C** February | |
| **4** Emilie | ☐ | **D** November | |
| **5** Mr. Drinkwater | ☐ | **E** July | |
| | | **F** January | |
| | | **G** December | |
| | | **H** June | |

| | A | B | C | D | E | F | G | H |
|---|---|---|---|---|---|---|---|---|
| **1** | ☐ | ☐ | ☐ | ☐ | ☐ | ☐ | ☐ | ☐ |
| **2** | ☐ | ☐ | ☐ | ☐ | ☐ | ☐ | ☐ | ☐ |
| **3** | ☐ | ☐ | ☐ | ☐ | ☐ | ☐ | ☐ | ☐ |
| **4** | ☐ | ☐ | ☐ | ☐ | ☐ | ☐ | ☐ | ☐ |
| **5** | ☐ | ☐ | ☐ | ☐ | ☐ | ☐ | ☐ | ☐ |

My progress: ☐ /5

**1** **Look at the three pictures.** Write the story shown in the pictures.
Write 35 words or more.

My progress: ___ /5

## 1 Order the words to make sentences.

1  rather / or outside? / eat / inside / Would / you

_____

2  strawberry jello / Daniela / prefers / to ice cream.

_____

3  rather / the / go / Facundo / would / to / movies.

_____

4  We / friends. / spend / with / to / prefer / time / our

_____

5  than / I'd / cabbage / rather / eat / soup.

_____

## 2 Complete the sentences with the past passive form of the verbs in the box.

> cook   ~~fry~~   give   make   not add   not tell

1  The mushrooms _____were fried_____ in oil.
2  The soup _____ with potatoes, broccoli, and cabbage.
3  Herbs _____ to the tortilla.
4  I _____ about the fire in the restaurant.
5  Sam _____ his grandmother's recipe.
6  The salmon _____ with onions.

## 3 Order the letters and write the words.

1  Can I have a **akset** _____ and **nooin** _____ sandwich, please?
2  I don't really like **delibo** _____ potatoes with my **tsaor** _____ lamb.
3  Put the **ciesdl** _____ apples, flour, sugar, and butter into the **sihd** _____ .
4  I usually **fyr** _____ **nomsla** _____ with oil and **cilrag** _____ .
5  Would you like a hot chocolate? I'll put the **elttke** _____ on the stove.

## 4 In pairs, answer the questions.

1  How is a cheese sandwich made? What do you need?

_____

2  Would you rather eat fast food or a traditional dish from your country?

_____

# 6 Environmentally friendly

## My goal

I can understand texts about the environment. **5**

## Mission Complete!

**3** I can read about how we keep our area clean.

I can write short emails and a story summary. **4**

I can understand the main points of a conversation. **2**

 **1** I can talk about environmental problems.

### And I need ...

### To do this, I will ...

### So I can ...

### I want to practice ...

 Diary

What I already know about the environment ...

What I have learned about the environment ...

## 1 Complete the text with the words in the box.

> air conditioning   a faucet   candles   ~~curtains~~   dishwasher   electricity
> heating   garbage   garbage can   lightbulbs   plugs   sink

Look what I found online! It's a beautiful treehouse. It's in Canada and it's made of wood. When you go inside, the first thing you see is the amazing windows. There are five! It's bright during the day, and at night, you can close the <sup>1</sup> _curtains_ .

There's <sup>2</sup> _____ and one or two <sup>3</sup> _____ , so you can use your laptops and tablets when you're there. It's nice and warm there in the winter because there's <sup>4</sup> _____ , but in the summer, it can get warm. There isn't <sup>5</sup> _____ , but the treehouse is in the trees, so it's never too hot.

If you want to make drinks and snacks, you can use the small kitchen area. There isn't a <sup>6</sup> _____ , but there's a <sup>7</sup> _____ with <sup>8</sup> _____ , so you can clean your cups and plates. It's important to remember that you're in the country there. If you don't want wild animals or insects to come in the treehouse, you have to put your <sup>9</sup> _____ in the <sup>10</sup> _____ !

At night, the bed is very comfortable and there's a lamp close to it so you can read. New <sup>11</sup> _____ are in the cupboard if you need them. It isn't a good idea to use <sup>12</sup> _____ , though. Remember the house is made of wood, and it's very high up!

## 2 🎧 5.17 Listen and check your answers.

## 3 Choose three items and write definitions. Say and guess in pairs.

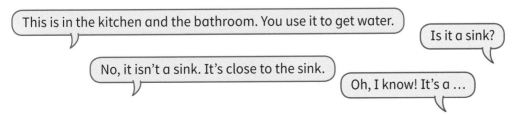

This is in the kitchen and the bathroom. You use it to get water.

Is it a sink?

No, it isn't a sink. It's close to the sink.

Oh, I know! It's a …

**1** **Read and complete the text.**

Last Christmas, I went [1]____to____ a small village called Jukkasjärvi [2]_____ Sweden [3]_____ my family. We stayed there [4]_____ three days and did lots of activities, like reindeer rides [5]_____ snowball fights. We spent one night in the amazing ice hotel! It's only open when it's very cold, so [6]_____ December to March or April. It's rebuilt every winter and looks different every time.

When you sleep in the ice hotel, you [7]_____ to wear very warm clothes because even the bed [8]_____ made from ice! I loved sleeping in the ice hotel, but I was very happy to sleep in a normal hotel in the next [9]_____. Would [10]_____ like to sleep in an ice hotel?

**2** 🎧 5.18 **Listen to the dialog.** Who has a vlog?

**3** 🎧 5.19 ⭐ **Listen. For each question, choose the correct answer. What is each person interested in at their hotel?**

| People | | Items | | | |
|--------|--|-------|--|--|--|
| 1 Helen | ☐ | **A** curtains | | **E** board games |
| 2 Isabella | ☐ | **B** electricity | | **F** swimming pool |
| 3 David | ☐ | **C** air conditioning | | **G** plug |
| 4 Victoria | ☐ | **D** movie theater | | **H** lightbulb |
| 5 Simon | ☐ | | | |

## ★ Grammar: *a lot of | lots of | a few | a little | many | much*

**1** **Choose the correct answer.**

1 We have put **a few** / **a little** candles on Sam's cake.

2 Are there **much** / **many** TVs in your house?

3 There's **a few** / **a lot of** garbage.

4 How **much** / **many** money do you want to spend?

5 I have **a little** / **many** chocolate in my bag. Do you want some?

6 Wow! There are **a few** / **lots of** famous people here today! I can see the whole Manchester soccer team …

**2** **Look and circle count and non-count.** Complete the sentences.

1 "Box" is **count** / **non-count**.

How ___many___ boxes are there?

2 "Ball" is **count** / **non-count**.

There are a _____ of balls.

3 "Sugar" is **count** / **non-count**.

How _____ sugar is there?

4 "Garbage" is **count** / **non-count**.

There's a _____ garbage.

5 "Rain" is **count** / **non-count**.

There isn't _____ rain in the desert.

6 "Panda" is **count** / **non-count**.

There are a _____ pandas.

**3**  **Listen and check your answers.**

**1** Find the environment words.

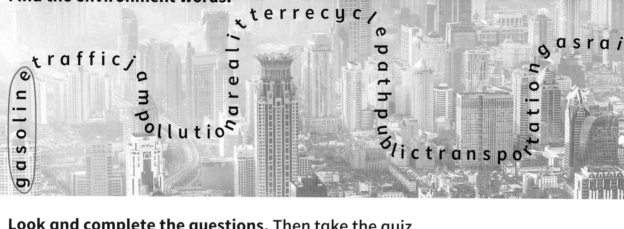

gasoline traffic jam pollution are a litter recycle path public transportation as rain forest

**2** **Look and complete the questions.** Then take the quiz.

**1** Which is the biggest
_____ in
the world?

**A** Amazon
**B** Sinharaja
**C** Daintree

**2** Where was the longest

_____

in history?

**A** Brazil
**B** India
**C** China

**3** Which of these three
cities has the most
expensive _____
(trains, buses, etc.)?

**A** Paris
**B** Shanghai
**C** London

**4** Which of these three
countries is the worst at
_____?

**A** South Korea
**B** the U.S.A.
**C** Germany

**5** What percentage
of Americans say
they have dropped
_____?

**A** 33%
**B** 43%
**C** 53%

**3**  5.21 **Listen to the quiz and check your answers.**

## ✪ Grammar: tag questions

**1** **Read and write the tag questions.**

1 Renata recycles all of her plastic,
   _doesn't she_ ?

2 You can't drive, _____ ?

3 That was a big traffic jam, _____ ?

4 You studied the rain forest last week,
   _____ ?

5 These are recycled bottles, _____ ?

6 Leonardo's never used the dishwasher,
   _____ ?

**2** **Read and complete the text.**

Wow, you're Harry Styles, [1] _aren't you_ ? You appeared on the
X Factor, [2] _____ ? That was in 2010, [3] _____ ?
You were in the group One Direction, [4] _____ ? You didn't win,
[5] _____ ? You were third. But now you're really famous! You've sold
lots of songs, [6] _____ ? But your band mate Zayn Malik
left in 2015, [7] _____ ? Oh, I'm asking too many questions,
[8] _____ ? I'm your biggest fan!

# Speaking 🎤

**3** ▶ **Watch Ezgi and Pablo doing some speaking practice. Complete the questions the teacher asks.**

1 Do _____ by car _____ ?

2 Is _____ where _____ ?

> **SPEAKING TIP!** Make sure you listen carefully and answer the questions.

**4** **Who doesn't answer a question correctly? Which question is answered?**

_____ doesn't answer a question correctly.
He/She answers the question:

A What causes pollution?

B Is pollution a problem in the capital city?

C Do you live close to an airport?

**5** 📋 **Now plan your answers to the questions in Activity 3.**

**6** ▶ **Watch the video again and listen. Underline where the stress falls in each of these words.**

1 comfortable      3 pollution

2 dirty            4 airport

> **PRONUNCIATION TIP!** Try to stress the most important words in the sentences.

**1** **Read the codex.** Write a sentence next to each picture to tell the story.

The king looked at the rain forest and

**2** 🎧 ⭐ **Listen.** For each question, write the correct answer in each blank. Write one
5.22    word or a number or a date or a time. You will hear the king talking to his
        people about taking care of the city.

### Clean up the city!

Start:        on <u>Saturday</u>   September   18th

For:          children from 7 to ¹_____ years old and all adults welcome

Meet:         at ²_____ a.m. in the main square

Activities:   learn about ³_____ and the animals in the area

Bring:        ⁴_____ and something to drink

**3** **Read an email from your friend, Richard.** Now write a reply. Write 25 words or more.

| ● ● ● ─. | | | | | |
|---|---|---|---|---|---|
| Home | Inbox | Sent | New | | 🔍 |

Hi,
What do you do to protect the environment in your area? Do you plant trees?
Do you recycle?

_____

_____

_____

_____

_____

_____

**1** Match the pictures to the names of the ecosystems.

Desert ecosystem

African grasslands ecosystem

Polar ecosystem

Rain forest ecosystem

**2** 🎧 5.23 **Listen to Ben talking about his grandparents' house.** Check the animals they have in their yard.

**1**

**2**

**3**

**4**

**5**

**6**

**3** 🎧 5.24 **Listen again and write *yes* or *no*.**

1  They recycle glass.  *yes*

2  In the summer, the house is kept cool. _____

3  Their yard is big. _____

4  They grow fruit trees in the yard. _____

5  They've seen fish in the pond. _____

6  The yard is dangerous for hedgehogs. _____

**4** Write the living things and the non-living things that you see when you come to school. Compare your lists in pairs.

_____

_____

**1** **Here are some pictures that show different places to live.** Do you like these different places to live? Talk with a partner and say why or why not.

**2** **Talk with a partner and answer the questions.**

Do you think towns are quiet?

Do you think an apartment building is boring?

Do you think a house in the country is interesting?

Do you think an apartment close to a supermarket is useful?

Do you think a house with a yard is nice?

Which of these places to live do you like best?

**3** **Talk with a partner. Ask and answer the questions.**

1 Would you prefer to live on your own or with your family? Why?

2 What kind of home would you like in the future?

| My progress: | | |
| --- | --- | --- |
| I understood and answered all the questions. ☐ | I understood and answered most of the questions. ☐ | I didn't understand all the questions and needed some help. ☐ |

**You visited your English-speaking friend, Ally, last Saturday in her new house.**

Write an email to Ally.

In the email:

- say something about the area where the house is
- tell Ally about your favorite room in the house
- ask Ally to visit you next weekend

Write **25 words** or more.

My progress: ☐ /5

## 1 Complete the sentences with the words in the box.

a few    a little    ~~a lot~~    a lot of    many    much

1  There are _____a lot_____ of candles on my grandma's cake. One for every year, and she's 70 today!

2  How _____ time do we have at the park?

3  There's _____ litter on the street. It's very dirty here.

4  Quick! There aren't _____ tickets left for the concert – only 20. Let's get ours now.

5  There are only _____ people in school this morning. Public transportation is very bad today.

6  There's only _____ milk left. I'll go and buy some more.

## 2 Match the sentence halves.

1  You're ten today,            a  was it?

2  It wasn't good for the environment,    b  do we?

3  You can't use the dishwasher,       c  weren't they?

4  We have no electricity,           d  aren't you?

5  They were recycled notebooks,       e  can you?

## 3 Make two sentences with tag questions.

It's hot today, isn't it?    We're going to win the game, aren't we?

## 4 The words in bold are in the wrong sentences. Write the correct word for each sentence.

1  I love living in this **candles**. There are lots of parks and stores. _____

2  Is the **litter** good where you live? _____

3  What do you do when you find **heating** on the ground? _____

4  It isn't a good idea to use **public transportation** close to curtains. _____

5  It's very cold today. Please put the **area** on. _____

## 5 Answer the questions.

1  Think of a polluted place or place with lots of litter where you live. What can people do to try to make it better?

_____

2  Name three things you can find in your bathroom.

_____

# Review ••• Units 5–6

## 1 Complete the sentences.

1 The dishwasher _____ emptied today. Whose turn was it?

2 You've never met Arda Turan, _____ you?

3 You _____ cook very well, can you?

4 Would you _____ walk or take public transportation?

5 There are a _____ onions in the kitchen, but we need more for the paella. We're cooking for all our neighbors!

6 Lokman prefers _____ sleep with the air conditioning off. He thinks it's too noisy.

## 2 ⦿ Underline the incorrect word. Then write the sentence correctly.

1 I'd <u>prefer</u> have chicken than tomato soup. *I'd rather have chicken than tomato soup.*

2 Bautista didn't eat meat since he was nine. _____

3 I have much homework to do today. _____

4 The mushrooms are sliced and then put them in the dish. _____

5 Guadalupe was put the bottles outside and they were recycled. _____

6 There's a lot of litter in the country by their house. _____

## 3 Complete the texts with the words in the box.

> bandage   broccoli   chili   ~~cut~~   garbage can   pollution
> public transportation   saucepan   slicing   traffic jam

1 I __cut__ my finger when I was _____ the _____ . It's a tiny cut, but it's a huge _____ !

2 I hate being in a _____ , but I don't want to ride my bike to school because the _____ is so bad. And the _____ is awful where I live, so I can't take a bus or train.

3 It was a disaster. I put too much _____ in the sauce and I burned the _____ . Daniel and I agreed that the best place for the meal was in the _____ .

**1** 📝 **Look at the three pictures.** Think about the story.

**2** **Read Lucy's story.** Complete the chart with the ideas in the story.

James and Sam saw a poster about a clean-up at their local park and thought it was a great idea to help the environment. They went to the park on Monday at 2 p.m. and saw some people putting litter in bags. There were some soda bottles, a few magazines, and even an old phone. While Sam was talking to James, he walked into the trash can. Behind the trash can, there was a strange object. The boys took the object to the museum.

| Who? | James |
|------|-------|
| What? | |
| When? | |
| Where? | |
| Why? | |

> You have to give as many details as you can. Think about the following question words when you are planning your answer: Who? What? When? Where? Why?

**3** **Use your notes from Activity 2.** Write a follow-up story. What happens next? Write 35 words or more.

# 7 Feeling it

## My goal

### Mission Complete!

I can understand a simple text about feelings. **5**

I can find important information in simple texts. **4**

I can describe how a person is feeling. **3**

I can talk about a simple problem. **2**

I can give advice. **1**

### Diary

What I already know about feelings …

What I have learned about feelings …

### And I need …

### To do this, I will …

### So I can …

### I want to practice …

**1** **Look and complete the sentences.**

1 We saw this kangaroo when we were in Australia. Doesn't it look relaxed?

2 He didn't agree with the referee's decision. He was really a_____d.

3 Carl was very e_____d when he fell into the lake!

4 What's the matter with Rufus? Is he b_____d?

5 Mateo looks m_____e. What happened?

6 I'm trying to be p_____e, but I don't want to go to the beach in November!

**2** **Read and complete the conversations.**

| amazing   interested   negative   worried |

**Martina:** How many views did your video get?

**James:** It had 20,000 in the first hour!

**Martina:** Really? 20,000 people watched you fall over. That is ¹_____ .

**Mr. Green:** Then in 1543, King Henry VIII got married to his sixth wife … Amy! Why aren't you listening?

**Amy:** Oh, I'm sorry, I love history, but I'm not ²_____ in King Henry's wives. I was bored after number three.

**Jenny:** We're going to Disney World this summer.

**Kim:** That sounds great! Why do you look ³_____?

**Jenny:** I hate planes. I'm really scared of flying.

**Ben:** I don't want to go to a new school. I don't want to make new friends. I don't want to …

**Dad:** Oh, Ben, try not to be so ⁴_____ . You can do lots of sports in your new school. That'll be great, won't it?

**3** **In pairs, say and guess the adjective.**

I'm sitting at a beach …

You're bored!

No, I'm not. I have a large lemonade in my hand … I'm listening to music …

I know! You're relaxed!

**1** 🎧 5.25 **Listen to the conversation.** What animal is mentioned?

**2** 🎧 5.26 **Listen to the conversation again.** (Circle) the adjectives you <u>don't</u> hear.

> amazed   annoyed   bored   embarrassed   interested   miserable
> negative   positive   relaxed   satisfied   worried

**3** 🎧 5.27 ⭐ **Listen again.** For each question, choose the correct answer.

**1** Julia is probably taking a quiz
  **A** on the Internet.
  **B** in a magazine.
  **C** in a book.

**2** If someone puts a spider on her shoulder, Julia
  **A** will laugh.
  **B** will shout.
  **C** will cry.

**3** If Oliver's visiting castles in the rain, he'll feel
  **A** relaxed.
  **B** miserable.
  **C** interested.

**4** In the quiz, there's a total of
  **A** two questions.
  **B** eight questions.
  **C** ten questions.

**5** If you're negative, you should
  **A** put a spider on your shoulder.
  **B** walk in the rain.
  **C** try something new.

**4** 🎧 5.28 **Listen to two more questions in the quiz.** Then write your own answers.

**5** **Write a quiz question using some of the adjectives.** Then ask and answer in pairs.

( Here's my quiz question … )

## ★ Grammar: *don't need to, have to, should, shouldn't, ought to*

### 1 Choose the correct answer.

1 You **don't need to** / **should** be embarrassed – we all call our teacher "Mom" sometimes!

2 You **should not** / **have to** bring your homework to school.

3 I think you **should** / **don't need to** say sorry to your sister. It was your fault.

4 David **has to** / **ought to** join the soccer team to get in shape. He's very good!

5 I **should** / **ought** remember to make my grandpa a birthday card.

6 You **ought to** / **should not** forget your digital camera for the school trip.

### 2 Read the sentences and match them to the pictures. Then complete with a modal verb from Activity 1.

1 You _____ wear a helmet. ☐

2 You _____ wear funny clothes if you want to be a clown. ☐

3 You _____ draw on the sofa! ☐

4 You _____ bring any cakes to my party. I've made lots! ☐

A

B

C

D

### 3 Look at the code and complete the text.

| A | B | C | D | E | F | G | H | I | J | K | L | M |
|---|---|---|---|---|---|---|---|---|---|---|---|---|
| ● | ■ | — | ▲ | ★ | ○ | ⬢ | ÷ | ✕ | ! | ? | = | $ |

| N | O | P | Q | R | S | T | U | V | W | X | Y | Z |
|---|---|---|---|---|---|---|---|---|---|---|---|---|
| @ | % | & | ✱ | < | > | // | ∧ | " | { | ] | ← | ↑ |

Dear Jenny,

Thanks for offering to take care of my dog, ¹// ✕ @ ←  __Tiny__ . You have to take her for a walk at least five times a day. She's always very hungry, so you ² > ÷ % ∧ = ▲ _____ give her lots of food and water every day. She ³ = ✕ ? ★ > _____ watching TV, so you ⁴ > ÷ % ∧ = ▲ @ % // _____ forget to put on her favorite TV shows.

See you next week.

Beatrice

P.S. She likes playing with phones, so you ⁵ % ∧ ⬢ ÷ // // % _____ keep your phone in your bag.

**1** Read and complete the texts with the words in the box.

| ache | breathe deeply | diet | exercise | gym | health | ~~jogging~~ | recover | stay in shape | stress |

**A**

**TRY A NEW SPORT**

Are you bored of going ¹ ___jogging___ around your local park? Then join our color run! The length of the race is five km, and you'll be covered in paint. It's awesome, but your legs will ² _____ the next day. When you ³ _____, you'll want to do it again and again!

**B**

# Have a laugh!

How many times have you laughed today? Not many? Laughter is the best way to reduce ⁴ _____ and it's a great way of doing ⁵ _____. So you can ⁶ _____ without going to the ⁷ _____!

**C**

## Top of your game

If you want to be a top athlete, it's important to take care of your ⁸ _____. You should eat the right foods and have a healthy ⁹ _____. No more cola and candy! To prepare for a race, you should practice, practice, practice. Then just before the race begins, ¹⁰ _____, look at the finish line and think about winning! Good luck!

**2** 🎧 5.29 Listen and check your answers.

**3** Ask and answer in pairs.

1 Would you rather do a color run or laugh with your friends? Why?

> I would rather …

2 How do you prepare for a big event when you're nervous?

> When I'm nervous before a big event, I …

## ★ Grammar: *such a … that / so … that*

**1** **Complete the sentences with *so* or *such* and *that*.**

1  James and Maria have ____such____ a tiny car ____that____ there isn't enough room for their kids!

2  I was _____ embarrassed on my first day at school _____ I couldn't remember my name.

3  It was _____ a cold day _____ we stayed inside and played card games.

4  My dog runs _____ quickly _____ I have to ride my bike next to him.

**2** **Complete the text with *so* or *such* and *that*.**

My hero is Ellie Simmonds. She's a British swimmer and she's won lots of swimming competitions. She was ¹____so____ young when she took part in her first Paralympic Games that she was still in school. She was only 13! She works ²_____ hard and is ³_____ a friendly person when she's on TV. She swam ⁴_____ fast at the Rio Paralympic Games in 2016 ⁵_____ she won a World Record! But there's one thing she doesn't want us to know – she has ⁶_____ a fear of lakes ⁷_____ she only swims in swimming pools!

# Speaking

**3** ▶ **Watch Pablo and Ezgi doing Phase 1 of the speaking practice.** Order the questions.

How much water do you like to drink? ☐

What about you? ☐

Do you like to sleep a lot? ☐

What do you think about spending a lot of time outside? ☐

Do you like going to the gym? ☐

Do you like to sleep a lot? ☐

**4** ▶ **Watch Phase 2 of the video.** Complete each sentence.

1  Now, what exercise do you _____, Pablo?

2  It's _____.

3  What do you _____, Ezgi?

4  I _____ about the problem.

**5** 📝 **Now plan your own answer to the question.**

1  What do you do to be healthy?

**SPEAKING TIP!** Ask your partner questions to involve them.

**PRONUNCIATION TIP!** In "wh" questions, the stress usually falls on the final word.

## 1 Read the story and answer the questions.

1 Why did the cowboys wake up?

They woke up because they heard a wolf.

2 Why was Cody so worried?

3 What did he decide he ought to do?

4 How did Buck feel about his new job?

5 Why did he shout "wolf"?

6 What happened when he shouted "wolf" the first two times?

7 Why was Blossom angry with her brother?

8 What happened at the end of the story?

## 2 Look and write notes. Tell the story in pairs.

One day, a hungry wolf dressed up as a calf.

**3** **Read and answer.** Write *yes* or *no*.

1  Cody was the youngest cowboy.  _no_

2  Buck stayed and took care of the calves.  ___

3  Buck was bored watching the calves.  ___

4  Buck shouted "wolf" because he wanted someone to talk to.  ___

5  There were wolves the second time Buck shouted "wolf."  ___

6  When there really were wolves, nobody came to help.  ___

**4** ⭐ **You want to visit Buck on the ranch.** Write a short note asking him about your visit.

In the note:

- ask where the ranch is
- say which animals you'd like to see
- say how you will travel there

Write **25** words or more.

## 1 Look and answer the questions.

1 How do you think each of these people are feeling?

2 How do you think you would feel in these situations?

3 What you could say to them to make them feel better?

## 2 Read and say what you would do.

### Situation 1

A friend asks you to a party. You find out that all of the girls in your group are invited except for Sara. How do you think she will feel when she finds out?

A angry     C annoyed     E worried

B sad     D embarrassed

Sara asks you, "Are you going to the party?" Choose what you might say to her:

A Yes, I'm going. Are you?

B Yes, everyone's going.

C Yes. I'm sorry you weren't invited. I think her parents said she could only invite a few people.

D Sorry, yes, I am. Is it true that you aren't going?

### Situation 2

You see your friend, Ben, in the morning and he is happy and smiling. After school, you see him again and he looks upset. What might have happened? Give reasons for your ideas.

A He had an argument with someone.

B He didn't do well on a test.

C Someone has been mean to him.

D He's just had a bad day.

## 3 🎧 5.30 Listen to the conversations. Who shows empathy?

## 4 🎧 5.31 Listen again and check the phrases you hear.

A Oh, that must be really upsetting for you. ☐

B I'm really sorry. Are you OK? ☐

C That's great news – I'm so glad. ☐

D Sorry. I didn't mean to hurt your feelings. ☐

E You look upset. Are you OK? ☐

F I know how you feel. ☐

**Skills practice**

**1** For each question, choose the correct answer.

## What should you read on vacation?
Here are our "Top 3" choices for this summer.

*Patty's Diary* (by Jennie Hills) follows the life of Patty Puller, now in her last year of school. What will happen when she leaves school? What about her neighbor Phillip? Who will continue to take care of her best friend, Florence? This is the third and final Patty Puller story.          Price $10.00

*Stolen Jewelry* (by Liz White) It's the 1940s and Lady Angela Bellefort is excited about staying at her grandmother's Irish castle for her birthday. After a strange accident, Angela suddenly loses her memory. However, she makes two new and unusual friends. Ron and Elsa help her find the truth about some family jewelry.          Price $9.99

*Fire through the Fog* (by Ralph Derby) is a fantastic story about 15-year-old Marian who is interested in a secret group. With her twin sister's help, Marian wears a costume to get closer to the gang's boss. She learns a lot about staying in shape because the gang exercises every day. They plan to meet another member of the group who didn't agree with the boss. Can Marian keep her identity safe?          Price $9.50

You won't be bored this summer! If you want a story about a journal, an e-book about history, or a story about luck, take our advice and download one of these ebooks to read this summer!

 ----Our "Top 3" list of terrible scary stories comes out next week.----

1   The article says Patty Puller

   A ☐ has started a new school.

   B ☐ is going to finish school soon.

   C ☐ has a best friend called Phillip.

2   Who are Ron and Elsa?

   A ☐ members of Angela's family

   B ☐ Angela's school friends

   C ☐ Angela's new friends

3   Why does Marian wear a costume?

   A ☐ to be like her sister

   B ☐ to learn more about someone

   C ☐ to help her sister

4   The article says the person reading

   A ☐ should get one of these ebooks to read on vacation.

   B ☐ might feel bored on vacation.

   C ☐ should read a history ebook.

5   Next week, the article will be

   A ☐ about a terrible ebook.

   B ☐ another list of summer stories.

   C ☐ about stories to make you feel scared.

My progress: ☐ /5

**1** 🎧 5.32 **Listen. For each question, choose the correct answer.**
**You will hear Janie talking to her aunt Monica about a gym.**

1  What does Janie need to write about?

A  the new gym

B  Heart Street

C  her school

2  Janie thinks $50 is

A  too expensive.

B  too cheap.

C  the usual price.

3  Who is Robert?

A  Janie's cousin

B  a school teacher

C  a friend of Janie's

4  Robert found it difficult to

A  stop eating candy.

B  start the running and good health class.

C  listen to his teacher.

5  Monica says the cycling class

A  happens once a month.

B  is enjoyable because of the music.

C  is always busy.

My progress: ___ /5

**7**

## 1 Complete the sentences with *don't need to*, *have to*, *should*, *shouldn't* or *ought to*. There may be more than one possible answer.

1 You _____ought to_____ drink water when you're jogging.

2 You _____ be quiet in a library.

3 We _____ take a coat to school today. It isn't going to rain.

4 You _____ speak to your parents if you're worried.

5 I _____ pack my bags tonight. I'm going on vacation tomorrow.

6 He _____ eat the curry. It's ten days old!

## 2 Order the words to make sentences.

1 he's / Josh / three / cold / sweaters. / that / is / so / wearing

Josh is so cold that he's wearing three sweaters.

2 I / fast / ache / ran / legs / today. / so / yesterday / my / that

_____

3 friendly / It / to / dog / is / say / that / hi. / such / a / stops / everyone /

_____

4 We / that / we're / so / 're / to / happy / going / cry.

_____

5 Alicia / fast / every / that / she / swimmer / is / wins / a / such / race.

_____

6 ten. / good / ten out / that / always / of / students / get / such / We're / we

_____

## 3 Complete the sentences with the words in the box.

> aches   annoyed   breathe deeply
> embarrassed   gym   healthy diet
> jogging   miserable   worried

1 I always feel relaxed after I've been to the _____ .

2 When you're _____ , don't shout. _____ instead.

3 She's _____ because her head _____ .

4 He's _____ because he fell over when he was _____ .

5 I was really _____ about my health, so I decided to eat a _____ and stay in shape.

## 4 Answer the questions in pairs.

1 What do you do to take care of your health?

2 How do you stay positive when you're stressed?

( To take care of my health, I always … )

# 8 Pretty cities

## My goal

I can read and understand information on posters.

**5**

## Mission Complete!

I can talk to my friends about things in the area outside school.

**3**

I can understand a range of original passages.

**4**

I can talk about different countries.

**2**

I can ask people to help me when I am traveling.

**1**

### And I need ...

### To do this, I will ...

### So I can ...

### I want to practice ...

 Diary

What I already know about cities ...

_____

_____

What I have learned about cities ...

_____

_____

**8**

## 1 Look and write the words in the crossword.

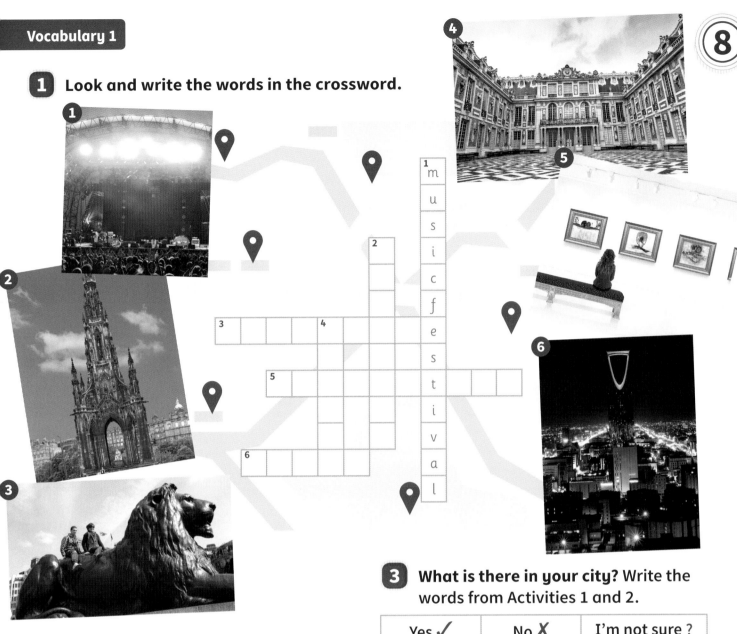

Crossword letters:
1 down: m u s i c f e s t i v a l

## 2 Read and complete the definitions.

1 Tourists go _____ around a city in a special vehicle. You can see the most interesting places very quickly.

2 A _____ is a big store, often with several floors. You can buy almost anything there!

3 A _____ is a building where you can see collections of paintings and other works of art.

4 A river _____ is a trip, often in the center of a city, where you don't travel on the roads. London, Paris, and Venice all have these.

## 3 What is there in your city? Write the words from Activities 1 and 2.

| Yes ✓ | No ✗ | I'm not sure ? |
|---|---|---|
|  |  |  |
|  |  |  |
|  |  |  |

## 4 Talk about your town or city.

**Katie** 🖤🖤

In my city, there are lots of sculptures. You can't go on a cruise because there isn't a river. But there is a music festival every summer. I love going there with my sister!

Unai's journal!
KEEP OUT!

**1** **Read Unai's journal.** Match the numbers (1–5) to the pictures.

Saturday

Dear Diary,

I'm so tired! Today my family and I visited all of our favorite places in Bilbao in just one day!

**1** 10:00 a.m.

First, we went to the Guggenheim Museum. It's a modern art gallery with lots of awesome paintings and you can buy lots of postcards there, too. But I prefer to look at the amazing sculpture which is next to the entrance. It's called *Puppy* and is ten meters tall. It's made of flowers, so it's different in the summer and winter!

**2** 12:00 p.m.

Afterward we went to see a sculpture of a giant metal spider that's next to the river. I love it, but my sister hates it because it looks pretty scary. She shouldn't worry – it doesn't bite!

**3** 2:00 p.m.

My brother loves sailing, so in the afternoon we visited the Maritime Museum. They have a big collection of model ships and boats. The museum is closed on Mondays, so if you want to go you should go on a weekend.

**4** 4:00 p.m.

Later, we went shopping in a department store downtown. My mom wanted to take the bus, but it's very close so we decided to go there on foot. If you like music, you can go there to book tickets for one of the concerts and festivals that are held in Bilbao every year.

**5** 6:00 p.m.

Finally, we took the train and went up the hill to Artxanda. You can see the city, the mountains, and the river from there. It's great for taking amazing pictures!

**2** ⭐ **Read the journal again.** Answer the questions.

1 Unai's favorite part of the museum is
   A the large sculpture.
   B the drawings.
   C the store.

2 Where did Unai go because of someone in his family?
   A a concert
   B the art gallery
   C the museum

3 How did Unai and his family get downtown?
   A They took the bus.
   B They walked.
   C They took the train.

4 What would Unai say about Bilbao?
   A There's not very much to do here – it's so boring!
   B It's difficult to see everything in just one day.
   C Only people who like music will enjoy my city.

## ⭐ Grammar: indirect questions

**1** **Read and complete the questions.**

1 How many paintings are there?   Do you know how many paintings _there_ _are_ ?
2 What can I see in Istanbul?   Do you know _____ in Istanbul?
3 Where is Sarah?   Can you tell me _____ ?
4 How much does this cost?   Can you tell me _____ ?

**2** **Find and write five sentences.**

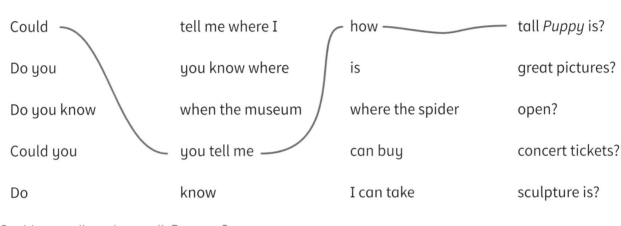

| | | | |
|---|---|---|---|
| Could | tell me where I | how | tall *Puppy* is? |
| Do you | you know where | is | great pictures? |
| Do you know | when the museum | where the spider | open? |
| Could you | you tell me | can buy | concert tickets? |
| Do | know | I can take | sculpture is? |

1 Could you tell me how tall *Puppy* is?
2 _____
3 _____
4 _____
5 _____

**3** **Read the journal on page 96.** Talk together and answer the questions.

> Could you tell me how tall *Puppy* is?

> Yes, he's ten meters tall. That's as tall as my school!

**4** 🎧 5.33 **Read the facts.** Which ones are true? Write *yes* or *no*. Then, listen and check.

a In the U.S.A., theme parks are more popular than museums.

b There are 100 bathrooms in Buckingham Palace.

c The Eiffel Tower is shorter in the winter.

**1** **Look at the code.** Write the words.

| A | B | C | D | E | F | G | H | I | J | K | L | M |
|---|---|---|---|---|---|---|---|---|---|---|---|---|
| ● | ■ | — | ▲ | ★ | ○ | ⬡ | ÷ | ✕ | ! | ? | = | $ |

| N | O | P | Q | R | S | T | U | V | W | X | Y | Z |
|---|---|---|---|---|---|---|---|---|---|---|---|---|
| @ | % | & | ✶ | < | > | // | ∧ | ‖ | { | ] | ← | ↑ |

1 You can buy tickets at the //%∧<✕>// ✕@○%<$●//✕%@ —★@//★<.

tourist information center

2 I got my map from the //%∧<✕>// ✕@○%<$●//✕%@ —★@//★<.

3 My mom looked at the gallery's %&★@✕@⬡ ÷%∧<> online.

4 We're in the &●<?✕@⬡ =%//, but we've lost our car!

5 My dad gave me some money from the —●>÷ $●—÷✕@★.

6 The >✕⬡@ says we should go left.

7 I dropped my ice cream on the >✕▲★{●=?!

8 It's really quick to use the >∧■{●←.

9 My mom's car got stuck in the //<●○○✕— —✕<—=★.

**2** 🎧 5.34 **Listen and write the numbers on the map.**

## ★ Grammar: *used to*

**1** **Find and write four sentences.**

| | | |
|---|---|---|
| ~~I used~~ | I didn't use | Which sports |
| hate broccoli | did you use | used to live |
| Shakira | to play? | When I was three |
| in Colombia | ~~to~~ | to do homework |

1  I used to _____

2  _____

3  _____

4  _____

**2** **Order the words to make sentences.**

1  world's / tallest / tower / used / to / The / in / New York. / be

_____

2  be / art / station. / used / to / This / a / train / gallery

_____

3  gold? / to / monument / use / this / be / Did

_____

4  People / cash / use / to / machines. / didn't / use

_____

## Speaking

**3** **Watch Ezgi and Pablo doing some speaking practice. Which questions does the teacher ask?**

1  Where do you live? ☐

2  Where do you come from? ☐

3  What's your name? ☐

4  What's your favorite town or city? ☐

**4** **Watch again and complete Pablo's answer.**

Well, I ¹_____ my town, Carmona, because it's a ²_____ place, but there are lots of things to do there. Tourists like to visit the ³_____ , which is a hotel now, and there are some interesting ⁴_____ , too. If you want to see a ⁵_____ Spanish town, I really recommend it.

**5** **Now plan and practice your answer to the questions with a partner.**

quiet place

My city

**6** **Watch the video again. Underline the stressed words in each question.**

1  Now, what's your name?

2  And how old are you?

3  Pablo, where do you live?

4  And Ezgi, where do you come from?

**PRONUNCIATION TIP!** In questions, the stress usually falls on the key word / most important piece of information.

**1** Label the contents of Johnny Ming's suitcase using the words from the box.

apple juice    black tie    ~~box of chocolates~~    clothes    racket    toothbrush

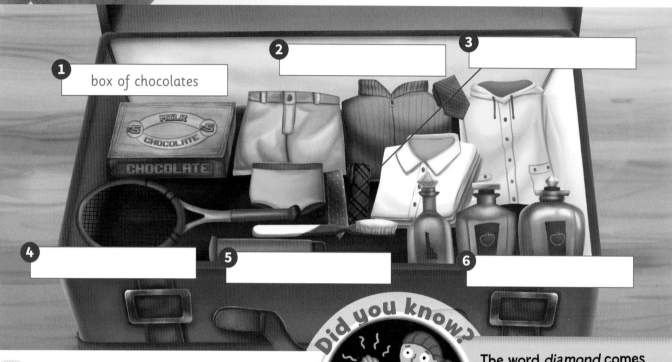

1  box of chocolates

**2** Why does Johnny Ming pack these things? Write your ideas below.

_____

_____

_____

**Did you know?**

The word *diamond* comes from the Greek word ἀδάμας (adamas) and means something that can't be broken. This is a good name because diamonds are one of the hardest materials on Earth!

**3** Read the story again and answer the questions.

1  What does Johnny Ming do from Monday to Friday?

He is China's Number One secret detective.

2  What is his secret job?

_____

3  Who does Huxley think has stolen the Butterfly Diamond?

_____

4  How do you think Johnny Ming feels when he finds Mia and Sami?

_____

5  What do Mia and Sami say they know?

_____

**For each question, choose the correct answer.**

Think about why someone has written a message. What is their reason for writing it?

## 1

**MING'S MARVELS**

I am not here this Saturday and Sunday. I am back on Monday morning at 9

See you then, my dear customers,
Johnny Ming

**Why has Johnny Ming written this notice?**

A   To tell his customers the store is closed on the weekend.

B   To tell his customers the store isn't open on Monday.

C   To tell his customers about where he is going.

## 2

Dear Mom,
Sami and I are going to stay with Aunt May this weekend. She is meeting us at the train station. I'll call you when we arrive.
Love, Mia

**Mia**

A   is asking if she can stay with her aunt.

B   is explaining that she is going to stay with her aunt.

C   is telling her mom that her aunt is coming to stay with them.

## 3

**THE BRITISH MUSEUM**

Coming soon: The Butterfly Diamond
See the world's most beautiful stone!

Full-price tickets for adults, children under 12 free

A   Children younger than 12 have to pay for a ticket.

B   No adults can see the Butterfly Diamond for free.

C   Children can see the Butterfly Diamond for free.

## 4

My dear Huxley,
Of course you can have the Butterfly Diamond. After all, it's yours! You only need to give me one thing: $100,000. You see – easy!
Your friend, Arabella

**Arabella**

A   is saying she won't give Huxley the Butterfly Diamond.

B   is saying she doesn't have the Butterfly Diamond.

C   is saying Huxley can pay lots of money to have the Butterfly Diamond.

## 5

**Your friend Greg has sent you an email asking you about things you used to do when you were younger, but don't do anymore.** Write an email to Greg. Write 25 words or more.

## 1 Read the texts about a national park.

**1** _____

Sumatra's largest national park offers the visitor adventure and excitement. Kerinci Seblat National Park stretches from the coastal plains of West Sumatra, up the forested valleys, and over the many rivers of the Barisan Mountains.

**2** _____

Kerinci Seblat is not a safari park with tourist buses or elephant rides. To enjoy the park, you have to hike and camp. Most visitors come to climb Gunung Kerinci (3,805m). It is the highest active volcano in Southeast Asia. The walk is difficult, but the views from the top are incredible. If you don't want to climb, you can explore the wetlands or visit caves that were lived in 9,000 years ago and see the cave paintings.

**3** _____

The most interesting feature of the park is its wildlife. It is home to 370 species of birds, elephants, bears, leopards, and tigers. The Sumatran tiger is an endangered animal, but their numbers have increased in Kerinci Seblat. Tourism is helping protect the park and in this way it is also helping to protect these beautiful big cats.

**4** _____

The local communities that live in the park have festivals all year long, and visitors are welcome. The most popular festival is called Kanuri Sko. In this festival, the villagers honor their ancestors with music, singing, and dancing.

**5** _____

It is very difficult to predict the weather in Sumatra, but the heaviest rains fall between December and February. The local people say that the best time to see tigers is after the rains. Remember that tigers are nocturnal and shy. It's very difficult to see them even after the rains, so don't be disappointed if you don't see one.

## 2 Read again and match the headings to the correct paragraphs.

> Local culture    Locations
> Sumatran wildlife    What to do
> When to go

## 3 Answer the questions.

1 What type of landscape can you find in Kerinci Seblat National Park?

_____

_____

2 How are tourists helping Sumatran tigers?

_____

_____

3 Do you think everyone would enjoy visiting this park? Why? / Why not?

_____

_____

**1** **For each question, choose the correct answer.**

# Department Stores

People who enjoy shopping like to find everything under one roof. Do you need some new <sup>1</sup>_____? Do you want to buy the latest video game or just have a <sup>2</sup>_____? The department store in Festival Place has everything including a restaurant if you need a break <sup>3</sup>_____ lunchtime or after school.

The store is open seven days a week. The parking lot is free <sup>4</sup>_____ it's only a five minute walk from the city center.

During the week, you can go to the movies and the amazing sports center which are on the first <sup>5</sup>_____. I asked my sister what she thought of the place. She said, "I never liked shopping before, but now I come <sup>6</sup>_____ at least once a week. It's great and the milkshakes in the café are amazing!"

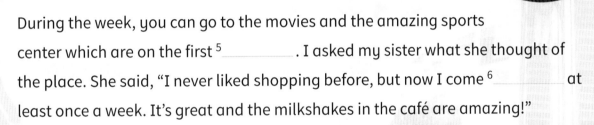

| | **A** | | **B** | | **C** | |
|---|---|---|---|---|---|---|
| 1 | A | chains | B | clothes | C | costumes |
| 2 | A | cup | B | drinks | C | coffee |
| 3 | A | at | B | in | C | on |
| 4 | A | if | B | or | C | and |
| 5 | A | floor | B | room | C | apartment |
| 6 | A | there | B | here | C | everywhere |

**1** **Read the review below and think of the word which best fits each blank.** Use only one word in each blank.

Write your answers IN CAPITAL LETTERS.

**Weekend Festival**

"FunTimes" is one of the best weekend festivals in August. I'll definitely go next summer, too. The great variety of activities is suitable ¹_____ all ages. There's a cake competition on Friday afternoon, and from 11 p.m. to 1 a.m. there's a Scary Stories event. Most kids wear their pajamas for that.

Everyone camps in campsites in the nearby fields so you never have ²_____ walk far for a performance. My only suggestion is don't camp too close to the main stage because ³_____ is live music all evening. The musicians are amazing, but they might keep you awake.

You'll need to book for some of the popular activities like Night Stars, ⁴_____ for everything else you can just show up at the last minute. Don't forget to try the delicious food, too, and ⁵_____ you forget to bring anything, you'll find it in the awesome store. The costumes for the Crazy Animals party ⁶_____ Sunday were the most interesting I've ever seen!

**1  Write five questions about your city.**

1  Where is the zoo?
2  _____
3  _____
4  _____
5  _____

**2  Now make the questions in Activity 1 more polite.** Use indirect questions.

1  Can you tell me where the zoo is, please?
2  _____
3  _____
4  _____
5  _____

**3  Match the sentence halves.**

| | | | |
|---|---|---|---|
| 1 | Jenny's grandmother didn't | **a** | be Nadal's coach? |
| 2 | I used | **b** | use to look for things on the Internet. |
| 3 | Did you use to | **c** | to share his video games with me. |
| 4 | My friend used | **d** | to listen to One Direction. |

**4  Now write sentences about when you were younger.** Remember to use *used to*.

**5  Complete the words in the sentences.**

1  You should walk on the s i d e w a l k , not the road.

2  Can you tell me where I can buy tickets for the
r ____ c _____ ? Yes, the t _____
i _____ c _____ is over there.

3  Go straight ahead to the t _____ c _____ ,
past the s _____ , and the p _____ l ____
is on your left.

4  There used to be a s _____ in front of the
g _____ , but it moved last year.

5  Do you know what time that d _____
s _____ closes? I'm not sure, but I think the
o _____ h _____ are on the door.

> My favorite place is the park because I can see my friends there.

**6  Read the questions and plan your answers.** Make notes then practice with a friend.

1  Where's your favorite place in your town?
2  What is there to do in your town on weekends?

# Review ••• Units 7–8

## 1 Choose the correct answer.

1 You **have to** / (**should**) say sorry to your sister. Why did you hide her favorite toy bear?

2 You **ought** / **should** to go to the Empire State Building when you're in New York, but only if you have time.

3 Pedro was **such** / **so** miserable when I saw him in the gallery.

4 Li was **such a** / **such** good friend to me when I started in this school.

5 I **use** / **used** to ride my bike on the sidewalk when I was little, but I don't now.

6 Could you tell me when the **last sightseeing tour is** / **is the last sightseeing tour** today?

7 Do you know **how many people work** / **work how many people** in the department store?

## 2 ⊙ Underline the incorrect word. Then write the sentence correctly.

1 Please listen carefully. I'm going to tell you what <u>should you</u> do.

   Please listen carefully. I'm going to tell you what you should do.

2 You have go to the gym more often if you want to be as strong as Hulk.

_____

3 You don't need do your homework tonight because it's the weekend.

_____

4 There use to be a tourist information center on King Street, but there isn't now.

_____

5 I used to was embarrassed when I sang, but now I don't mind.

_____

6 I should to go to bed now.

_____

## 3 Complete the words and then match them to the pictures.

 A
 B
 C
 D
 E
 F

1 t _ a _ f _ c   c _ r _ l _  ☐

2 s _ u _ p _ u _ e  ☐

3 c _ l _ b _ i _ y  ☐

4 c _ r _ o _ n  ☐

5 w _ r _ i _ d  A

6 r _ l _ x _ d  ☐

⑧

**1 Read this email from your English-speaking friend Louise.**

Me, too!

> Hi!
> I'm so excited that you're visiting me this weekend. I have lots of exciting ideas!
> First, let's go on a sightseeing tour. There's a bus that drives around all the interesting sights. Then, we can either climb up the tower and see the whole city, or go shopping in the new department store. It's enormous! What would you rather do?
> In the evening, we ought to go for a walk by the river with my family. It's really nice in the summer, and there are lots of nice restaurants. Where would you like to eat?
> Anyway, could you tell me what time your train arrives? I'll meet you at the station!
> See you soon!
> Louise

Tell Louise

Tell Louise what time

Suggest types of restaurants you like

**2 Underline Louise's questions. Make short notes to answer Louise's questions.**

> You have to answer all the questions in the email. It's a good idea to underline the questions before you make notes.

_____

_____

_____

**3 Now write your answer to Louise in about 100 words.** Use your notes in Activity 2 to help you.

# 9 Lights, camera, action!

## My goal

**Mission Complete!**

I can express imagination. 5

I can write a simple story. 3

I can write an email to a friend. 4

I can understand advice. 2

I can talk about movies. 1

**And I need …**

**To do this, I will …**

**So I can …**

**I want to practice …**

## Diary

What I already know about TV and movies …

What I have learned about TV and movies …

**1** **Order the letters and write the words.**

1  rcaootn _____    3  madar _____    5  mage  oswh _____

2  moyecd _____    4  eht  ensw _____

**2** **Take the quiz.** Find out the best program for you.

**1** **Yay, it's the weekend! What are you going to do this morning?**

Go to a museum. I want to learn more about Egypt.

Turn on my phone and check my messages.

This morning? I sleep all day and I'm awake all night on weekends!

I'm already at the gym!

**2** **Complete this sentence. "It's late at night. Sophie hears a noise, turns around and …**

says, "What a pretty mouse! What type of mouse are you?"

screams at the big, dark monster with two heads.

sees a helicopter flying toward her.

takes her camera and notebook from her bag.

**3** **Your teachers say that …**

you're good at art, but your paintings are scary!

your best subject is P.E.

you work hard and always do your homework.

you're popular, but you shouldn't talk so much in class.

**4** **Who would you like to have dinner with?**

Rosario Flores      Albert Einstein

Prince Harry        Frankenstein

**5** **Choose your favorite vacation.**

**Mostly yellow:**
You should watch a documentary.
**Mostly green:**
You should watch a talk show.
**Mostly pink:**
You should watch a horror movie.
**Mostly blue:**
You should watch an action movie.

**1** **You are going to listen to four short texts.**
**Look at the pictures and guess what they're about.**

I think the first text is about …

**2** 🎧 5.35 ⭐ **Listen. For each question, choose the correct answer.**

**1** You will hear two friends talking about a trip to the movie theater.

What did they both like about the movie?

**A** the ending

**B** the main character

**C** the parts where there was fighting

**2** You will hear two friends talking about a news story.

What happened to the girl in the story?

**A** She was missing in the jungle for five days.

**B** She was injured by a monkey.

**C** She was rescued by the police.

**3** You will hear two people talking about a game show.

Which topic was the most difficult?

**A** popular songs

**B** languages around the world

**C** history

**4** You will hear two people discuss a program they watched last night.

What do they both agree on?

**A** Something horrible would happen.

**B** That sort of thing wouldn't happen in real life.

**C** The dog didn't want to be saved.

## ⭐ Grammar: causative *have/get*

**1** **Complete the sentences with the correct form of *have/get*.**

1  I _____have_____ my hair cut every month.

2  Tim and Anna _____ their pictures taken at the party last night.

3  Kelly is _____ her computer fixed right now.

4  We will _____ a pizza delivered tonight.

5  Paulo _____ his phone stolen yesterday.

6  You can _____ your birthday cake made in the new bakery.

**2** **Look and complete the sentences.** Use *have* or *get* and the word in parentheses.

1  _____ your car _____ here!
   (wash)

3  Clive the Crocodile _____ his teeth _____ once a year! (brush)

2  _____ your presents _____ by our friendly elves. (wrap)

4  I might _____ my nails _____ yellow. (paint)

**3** **Answer the questions.**

1  Have you ever had your face painted?

_____

2  Where do you get your hair cut?

_____

3  Do you always have your dinner cooked for you?

_____

**4** **In pairs, complete the sentences with your own ideas.**

1  I'd like to have my picture taken with …

2  I'd like to have a meal cooked by …

3  I'd like to have a … costume made for me.

**1** Find the television words.

review scene hero celebrity channel interview series program studio commercial performance

**2** Read and complete the texts with the correct form of the words in Activity 1.

Do you know what I hate? When I'm reading something online and a ¹ _commercial_ pops up. I don't want to listen to a ² _____ telling me to buy something. At least when I'm watching a ³ _____ on TV, I can change the ⁴ _____ .

If you don't know what movie to watch at the movie theater, watch a ⁵ _____ online first. You can watch movie fans in an ⁶ _____ about their favorite stars, and actors in a movie ⁷ _____ talking about their ⁸ _____ .

**3** Read and write the words in the crossword. Use the yellow letters to make the mystery word.

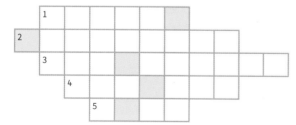

**1** When there's more than one episode, it's a …

**2** David Beckham is a … Everybody knows him!

**3** If companies want you to buy their things, they use … on TV, radio, or online.

**4** If you don't like a program on one …, you can choose a different one.

**5** A … is someone who does something amazing in a movie or book.

The mystery word is …

## ⭐ Grammar: second conditional

**1** **Complete the second conditional sentences with the verbs in parentheses.**

1  If I _____met_____ a spider with two heads, I _____'d be_____ terrified! (meet / be)

2  If Alex _____ a movie director, he _____ to Los Angeles. (become / move)

3  If you _____ good at quizzes, _____ on a game show? (be / go)

4  You _____ English if you _____ in China. (not speak / live)

5  Rosie _____ the horror movie if it _____ night time! (watch / not be)

6  _____ a cartoon if you _____ draw? (make / can)

**2** **In pairs, answer the questions so they are true for you.**

1  If you met a dog that could speak, what would you ask it?

2  If you had a robot, what would you get it to do?

3  If you could be a celebrity for a day, who would you be?

> If I met a dog that could speak, I would ask it what it thinks of cats!

## Speaking 🎤

**3** ▶ **Watch Ezgi doing some speaking practice.** Write the locations.

**SPEAKING TIP!** Remember to describe what you can see in all parts of the picture.

at the _____

in the _____

on the _____

on the _____

at the _____

**4** **Imagine you are Pablo.** In pairs, describe the picture.

**5** ▶ **Watch Pablo describe the picture.** Do you have the same ideas?

**PRONUNCIATION TIP!** When you ask more than one person the same question, the stress moves to the next person.

**1** Read the first four verses of the poem again. List the ways the writer makes the TV sound like a person.

The writer says the TV waits and waits. _____

_____

_____

_____

_____

**2** Check the positive things the writer says about children who didn't watch TV in the past.

In the writer's opinion, before the invention of TV, children …

were healthier. ☐                 played outdoors. ☐

read more. ☐                      had more fun. ☐

did more exercise. ☐             were more sociable. ☐

**3** Read the poem again and find the words that rhyme.

nose ___knows___

black _____

stare _____

bed _____

wings _____

floor _____

mind _____

square _____

alone _____

television _____

**4** Read and say what the writer's advice is to the reader.

1   Children should not watch a lot of TV, but it's OK to watch it sometimes.

2   Children should never watch TV because it's bad for them.

3   Instead of watching so much TV, children should spend their time doing more creative things.

**5** Make a list of the positive things about TV.

It's fun.

**6**  **Choose one verse.** Change it and write your own ideas about the "monster."

**7** 5.36 **Listen.** For each question, choose the correct answer.

**1** How did the boy hear about the movie?

A ☐

B ☐

C ☐

**2** What time are the friends planning to meet?

A ☐

B ☐

C ☐

**3** What would the woman like to have done?

A ☐

B ☐

C ☐

**4** What type of movie are they going to watch?

A ☐

B ☐

C ☐

**5** Where are they going to put the new TV?

A ☐

B ☐

C ☐

**6** What did the boy do last weekend?

A ☐

B ☐

C ☐

**1** **Describe the pictures.** Use the following words: *optical illusion, timing, perspective, proportion, scale.*

optical illusion

scale

timing

perspective

proportion

**2** **In pairs, talk about how the photographer has achieved the optical illusions in Activity 1.**

**3** **Take a picture of an optical illusion.** Write about how you achieved it.

**1** **Look at the three pictures.**

Write the story shown in the pictures.

Write 35 words or more.

My progress: ☐ /5

**1** **Answer the question.** Write your answer in about 100 words.

**Read this email from your English-speaking friend Sahar and the notes you have made.**

Sounds interesting!

Yes – say when

Hi!

Our drama teacher has given us a new project to do. Our group has to film a news program.

Could you help me prepare a news report about a TV show before Friday?

I thought either a comedy show or a documentary. Which would you prefer?

Is there anything you think we'll need to prepare the report?

Let me know.

Thanks,

Sahar

Tell Sahar

Suggest something to bring

**Write to your friend Sahar and use all of the notes.**

**1** Complete the sentences with the correct form of *have* or *get* and a word in the box.

dye   fix   make   ~~paint~~   steal   take

1   My grandparents are ___having___ their kitchen ___painted___ .

2   I _____ my laptop _____ yesterday. It works now!

3   We're going to _____ a big cake _____ for our party.

4   I _____ my hair _____ red, white, and blue. Do you like it?

5   We're _____ our picture _____ by a professional photographer tomorrow.

6   We _____ our luggage _____ at the station. We had to go to the police.

**2** Match the two sentence halves.

1   If you watched the movie,          a   you'd scream.

2   If you watched the horror movie,    b   you'd be very happy.

3   You'd be bored                      c   you'd know what happened.

4   If you met Ed Sheeran,              d   if you upset your best friend.

5   You wouldn't like candy             e   if you ate it every day.

6   You'd say sorry                     f   if you stayed at home all day.

**3** What was the last thing you had fixed?

_____

**4** Complete the two second conditional sentences.

If I found $1,000, I _____ .

I _____ if I had _____ .

**5** Complete the words in the sentences.

1   I watched an i n t e r v i e w with my
    h_____ , Zoella. I love her vlogs.

2   T___ n_____ is on c_____ 4 at
    7 p.m. every evening.

3   The r_____ of the a_____ m_____
    was very positive.

4   I didn't think his p_____ in the
    h_____ m_____ was very good.

5   The s_____ was silent when the
    g_____ s_____ began.

# 10 Review unit
## Units 1–3

**1** **With a partner, write a letter to the newspaper.** Choose a team, and then use ideas below to convince people to come and support the team.

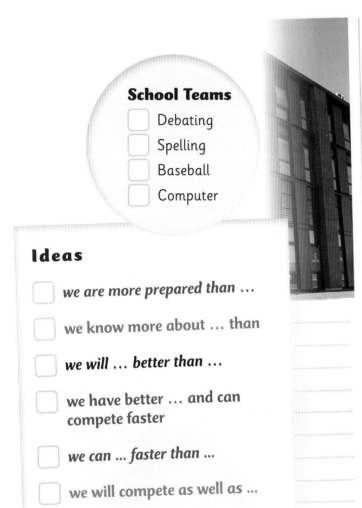

**School Teams**

☐ Debating
☐ Spelling
☐ Baseball
☐ Computer

**Ideas**

☐ *we are more prepared than ...*

☐ we know more about ... than

☐ *we will ... better than ...*

☐ we have better ... and can compete faster

☐ we can ... faster than ...

☐ we will compete as well as ...

Dear All-Star School Newspaper,

Our school has an amazing

_____ team. Come

watch our team compete at school because

_____

_____ .

In addition, we _____

_____ .

Finally, I think you should come support us

because _____

_____ .

Best wishes,

Tom, captain of the _____ team.

**2** **Find and (circle) the words.**

| bat | click | computer |
| download | hit | install |
| label | suit | tie |

```
C O M P U T E R H
L A B E L I R M I
I S U I T E B A T
C H I N S T A L L
K D O W N L O A D
```

**3** 🎧 5.37  **Listen and check (✓).**

| 1 | ☐ a mouse | ☐ b cell phones | ☐ c software | ☐ d screen |
|---|---|---|---|---|
| 2 | ☐ a mouse | ☐ b keyboards | ☐ c printers | ☐ d programs |
| 3 | ☐ a screen | ☐ b cell phone | ☐ c mouse | ☐ d disk |
| 4 | ☐ a laptop | ☐ b cell phone | ☐ c software | ☐ d keyboard |
| 5 | ☐ a mouse | ☐ b printer | ☐ c flash drive | ☐ d email |
| 6 | ☐ a laptops | ☐ b disks | ☐ c hardware | ☐ d screen |

**4** **Read and write *yes* or *no* .**

1 If you box, you need a raincoat. _____
2 If you play ice hockey, you need a racket. _____
3 If you play baseball, you need a bat. _____
4 If you go surfing, you need jewelry. _____
5 If you go biking, you need a bike. _____

**5** **Read. Circle the correct words.**

1 The sweater **will** / **need** look nice on you because it matches your pants.
2 **Could** / **Should** you find a leather purse in the last store?
3 If you want the blouse, you **should** / **will** try it on now because it's so pretty it will be gone soon!
4 I **would** / **might** buy a raincoat today if I felt like going shopping.
5 **Could** / **Would** you find any pretty jewelry in the department store display today?

**6** **Read. Write sentences using "If …."**

If you play soccer, you will have fun!

1 play soccer / have fun
2 bike too much / get tired _____
3 waterski / get wet _____
4 box / get hit _____

**7** Change sentences from passive to active.

1 An exciting game of ice hockey was played by two teams this morning.

   *Two teams played an exciting game of ice hockey this morning.*

2 The children are encouraged by their coach to practice soccer during the week.

   _____

3 The boy's bat was broken when Tom's super fast ball hit it.

   _____

4 Kids were carried far by the big waves as they surfed in the ocean.

   _____

5 When a new sports store was opened by our old coach, we all went to see it.

   _____

**8** 🎧 5.38 Listen and choose answers. Then discuss the question with a partner.

## MY DREAMS ...

Right now I'm only 11, but when I grow up, I am going to set a record for swimming. If I wear a high-tech lycra swimsuit, I will be able to [1]**win competitions / go much slower / have cool clothing**. And if I practice really hard, I will be in better shape [2]**than other people / than I want to be / than my dog**. I want to practice, so I can swim [3]**as fast as / than / as slow as** a dolphin!

In school, I am fast at writing. If I try hard, I write [4]**faster than my classmates / better than my classmates**. My teacher tells me writing well is [5]**rather than / more than / better than** writing fast. Do you think so?

**9** Complete the sentences. Then swap and read your partner's answers.

1 Can you _____ as fast as a bullet train?

2 George wants to be _____ than the world's biggest bodybuilder.

3 Would you want to _____ faster than a monkey?

4 Do you _____ ?

**10** Look at Activity 9. Write an answer to the question.

Think about *your* dreams. What would you do if you could do anything?

If I could do anything, I would _____ .

**11** **Read and complete the movie summaries.** Discuss your answers with a partner.

> could   may   might   should   will   would

## This month we're celebrating sports!

1. ***The Secrets of Expert Divers*** uses real videos of divers in Acapulco, Mexico. Don't miss this! You _____ see people dive from cliffs 29 m above the water.

2. ***Wonder Mouse Goes Water Skiing*** _____ be at the top of your list to see. "Wonder Mouse" Katie is super shy and scared of everything. That is until she takes a big leap … into waterskiing! Everybody is surprised at how she performs, and you _____ be, too.

3. ***Robert's Soccer Adventures*** is the hot number one box office hit! If you like soccer and learning about the world, then there's no doubt you _____ like this movie, too. Robert joins a traveling soccer team that competes all around the world in Italy, Spain, France, Mexico, China, Korea, and Japan! If you're learning about other countries in school, you _____ suggest seeing it as a class trip. ☺

**12** 🎧 5.39 **Listen and read.** (Circle) the wrong equipment and underline passive verbs.

*Al Does Sports* Movie Review
By Rebecca Hart

*Al Does Sports* is a very funny movie. Al is a skinny, very tall kid in high school. He tries all kinds of sports to be popular, but he's confused about what he should use for each sport. He buys a surfboard and racket to bike in a race. He is the slowest person in the race and crosses the finish line waving his racket in the air ten minutes after a 109-year-old cyclist. He is given a bat and buys a soccer ball to try baseball. He runs with the bat around the bases. Then he remembers he still has the bat at third base, drops it, gets tripped up, and tagged out! Finally, he buys a helmet and a purple polka-dotted swimsuit and plays golf. This is a sport that he does well in even wearing the wrong clothes! He wins many golf competitions, starts wearing normal golf clothes, and his whole life changes. I give it an excellent rating. It was so much fun!

**13** **Look at Activity 12.** Write about a sport you like to do or watch.

**14** **How are you doing?** Talk with a partner. Discuss and write.

| Things I am good at | Things I can improve |
|---|---|
|  |  |
|  |  |
|  |  |

# Units 4–6

**1** **Circle the words in the box. Label the pictures.**

> aspirin   bandage   boil   brain   bulb   cabbage   curtain   cut   dishwasher
> faucet   fry   garbage   lamb   pill   rest   salmon   sink   slice   steak

```
D H L S H J E Q J Q Q B J T F
T C B W I G A R B A G E S L A
L J A N E N P G Y Q Q P A G U
K I S I U P K G H A L M L C C
A R P V G Y S P R K Q Z M U E
K D I S H W A S H E R K O T T
U Y R J L D J L U N S F N H U
I A I L B I O V K U M T X T H
B I N M A R C M V B B D M E A
I J A M N S T E A K U R Q U T
D L K V D D D S P I L L A W M
C U R T A I N F K B E M B I D
F V S A G J N R H F O V G Z N
G D T E E Q G Y Y D W I I J B
D C A B B A G E C U U S L K G
```

**1**

**2**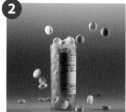

**3**

**4**

**5**

**6**

**2** **Look at Activity 1. Sort words by topic and complete the chart.**

| Food and cooking | Health | Household things |
|---|---|---|
| cut | | |
| | | |
| | | |
| | | |
| | | |
| | | |
| | | |

**3** **Unscramble the sentences and answer.** Then match to the pictures.

**1** watch a horror movie / to / Would / prefer / you / or a comedy?

Would you prefer to watch a horror movie or a comedy?

I would prefer to watch a comedy!

Picture: _e_

**2** the Earth, / You / to litter / don't like / do you?

_____

_____

Picture: ____

**3** salmon and broccoli / rather / Would / you / steak and potatoes / have / or / for dinner?

_____

_____

Picture: ____

**4** should all / We / , shouldn't we? / recycle more

_____

_____

Picture: ____

**5** or / have a / Would / you rather / dishwasher / an air conditioner ?

_____

_____

Picture: ____

**6** this evening / Would you / lamb with garlic and chili / herbs and mushrooms / prefer / or ?

_____

_____

Picture: ____

**a**

**b**

**c**

**d**

**e**

**f**

**4** **Complete the sentences with words from the box.**

> chili   don't you   garlic   have an operation   hospital
> pain   resting   salmon   steak   your visit

Dear Aunt Jenny,

I am going to the hospital to ¹ _____ this Friday. Have you ever had an operation? I've never even been in the hospital before, so it's new for me and kind of scary!

My parents are letting me take it easy before the operation, so I have been ² _____ and watching a lot of TV at home. Luckily I'm not in ³ _____ right now.

Being at home is a little boring, so I'm going to do some cooking. I love food with a lot of ⁴ _____ and ⁵ _____! Speaking of cooking though, you know my best friend's mom is a chef at the ⁶ _____, didn't you? She's coming to cook for me, and I know the food will be great. She told me I can have a choice of salmon with mushrooms and onions or ⁷ _____ with broccoli. I think that's pretty good, ⁸ _____? Since I prefer fish, I am going to have ⁹ _____. Which food would you choose, Aunt Jenny?

Honestly, I wish I could have pizza from my favorite local pizzeria, but I can eat that every night after I get home from the operation!

I'm looking forward to ¹⁰ _____ and catching up on all your news.

Love,

Clare

P.S. Here's a picture of me being a couch potato!

**5** **Look at Activity 4.** Underline three questions that Clare asks.

**6** **Ask your partner to dictate an email reply from Aunt Jenny.**
Write it, then swap. Answer Clare's questions.

Dear Clare,

_____

_____

_____

Love,

Aunt Jenny

**7** **Read.** Check the correct sentences.

1 ☐ **a** I was eating a lot of chili for the past week because my mom has been testing different recipes for a chili competition.

☐ **b** I have been eating a lot of chili for the past week because my mom has been testing different recipes for a chili competition.

2 ☐ **a** Adam has been resting from his knee operation for a few weeks, and he's had more time to hang out with his teammates than usual!

☐ **b** Adam was resting from his knee operation for a few weeks, and he's been having more time to hang out with his teammates than usual!

3 ☐ **a** Lily was using an air conditioner all the time since the summer started because it has been very hot and humid, and her curly hair gets more messy than a bird's nest in this weather.

☐ **b** Lily has been using an air conditioner all the time since the summer started because it has been very hot and humid, and her curly hair gets more messy than a bird's nest in this weather.

4 ☐ **a** Bob was boiling a lot of cabbage since yesterday when he found out his brother doesn't like the smell because he's very mad at his brother for breaking his computer by accident.

☐ **b** Bob has been boiling a lot of cabbage since yesterday when he found out his brother doesn't like the smell because he's very mad at his brother for breaking his computer by accident.

**8** **Read and cross out the words that do not belong for each topic.** Then write them in the correct category.

**Health and medicine**
heart, operation, rain forest, rest, pollution, accident, feel better, feel sick, fever, pain, dishwasher, stress, public transportation, _____ , _____ , _____ , _____ ,

**Food and cooking**
curtain, broccoli, herbs, aspirin, lamb, cabbage, mushroom, oil, onion, steak, prescription, boil, pot, frying pan, operation, salmon, _____ , _____ ,

**Home and the environment**
litter, injure, gas, recycle, lamb, air conditioning, light bulb, heating, flu, sink, garlic, _____ , _____ , _____ , _____ ,

**9** **Use as many words as possible from the charts above to write your own sentences.**

1 For dinner, my mom is going to cook either lamb or steak with broccoli, mushrooms, onions, and herbs.

2 _____

3 _____

# Units 7–9

True??? False???

**1** **Read and write** *yes* **or** *no*.

1 If you are lost, you should get help with directions. _____

2 If you didn't use to eat healthily, you can always start to eat better any time. _____

3 If you want to go to a museum, you don't need to go when it is open. _____

4 If you feel happy doing something, you might want to do it again. _____

5 If you are trying something new, you shouldn't pay attention or try hard. _____

**2** **Write your own** *yes* **or** *no* **sentences.** Read to your partner and let them guess.

1 _____

2 _____

3 _____

**3** **Read and correct the advice.** Then match the sentences to the pictures.

1 If you weren't happy you got invited to that party, you should go!

If you weren't happy you got invited to that party, you **shouldn't** go! _____

2 If you aren't a fan of scary monsters, you should go see the latest monster horror movie.

If you aren't a fan of scary monsters, _____.

3 If Steve were to get lost sightseeing in a big city, he shouldn't ask for directions.

If Steve were to get lost sightseeing in a big city, _____.

4 If Pam were to get praised for her documentary, she shouldn't feel satisfied.

If Pam were to get praised for her documentary, _____.

**a**   **b**   **c**   **d**

**4  Complete these sentences and match to the pictures.**

1  If I were embarrassed I didn't have enough money for tickets to the art gallery, I would

_____ .

2  If I were feeling annoyed about long lines at a museum, I would _____ .

3  If I were worried about taking the subway alone, I would _____ .

4  If I were interested in traveling somewhere in the world, I would _____ .

**a**

**b**

**c**

**d**

**5  Match. Then make four of your own sentences and tell a partner. Then swap.**

1  When you are feeling relaxed,     **a**  you should talk about it with a friend.

2  When you are miserable,     **b**  you should check the cruise times first.

3  When you are feeling sick,     **c**  people will try to take your pictures a lot.

4  When you are a celebrity,     **d**  you should go to the tourist information center.

5  When you are going sightseeing,     **e**  it's easier to deal with stressful problems.

6  When you are going on a river cruise,     **f**  you should lie down and rest.

**6** **Read the questions and write answers.**

1　If you could be in a talk show, a comedy, or a game show, which would you choose? Why?

　If I could choose, I would _____

　_____ .

2　If you could be a hero of a thriller, a drama, or an action movie, which would you choose? Why?

　If I could choose, I would _____

　_____ .

3　If you could meet a movie or TV star, who would you choose? Why?

　If I could choose, I would _____ .

4　If you could go sightseeing on a river cruise, in a tour bus, or walking on foot, which would you choose? Why?

　If I could go, I would _____ .

5　If you could visit a museum, a tower, or a monument, which would you choose? Why?

　If I could choose, I would _____ .

6　If you could go anywhere in the world, where would you go? Why?

　If I could choose, _____ .

**7** **Look at Activity 6 again.** Then compare and discuss answers with a partner.

If you could visit a museum, a tower, or a monument, which would you choose? Why?

If I could visit a museum, a tower, or a monument, I'd choose a tower. I'd want to go and see the funniest tower in the world!

## 8 Choose an ending for each sentence.

> even the director is embarrassed    her house is like a palace    I laugh each time I think of it
> it took up ten rooms    planes can see it when they fly by    the saleswoman asked him to leave
> the theater is packed every night    we returned in the dark

1   The monument by the tourist information center is so tall that _____ .

2   The sightseeing river cruise was so long that _____ .

3   Lady Burn's art collection is so large that _____ .

4   Celebrity Tina Foy is so rich that _____ .

5   The horror movie has been such a big hit that _____ .

6   The documentary was such a disaster that _____ .

7   The comedy was so funny that _____ .

8   Her grandfather was so rude at the store that _____ .

## 9 Look at the pictures. Complete the sentences using your own ideas.

The sculpture is a cherry on a spoon. It is so _____ that _____ .

The sculpture weighs 18,000 kg and is 13 m high. It has such a _____ that _____ .
The artist modeled it on his own thumb!

This puppy dog sculpture is a 13 m tall living topiary. This "growing" sculpture is so tall that gardeners _____ .

## 10 Look at Activity 9.

1   Which is your favorite sculpture? Why? _____

2   If you could make a really big sculpture, what would you make? Why?
_____

# Home Booklet

Paul Drury

**CAMBRIDGE**
UNIVERSITY PRESS

# 1 In style

**Skim the text and find:**

1  four animal names

_____

2  four different materials we use for clothes

_____

## Looking good!

Take a look at what you're wearing. What's it made of? Where did it come from? Even if your T-shirt is brand new, it's probably traveled a lot farther than you will in your whole life.

It's cold, you wear a sweater. Maybe that sweater is made out of cotton or polyester; maybe it's made out of wool. Where did that wool come from? Sheep? Yeah, there's a good chance of that. Camel? Possibly. Goat? Why not? Rabbit? Could be. Some type of cow? Yep. Our ancestors were very practical and made good use of what they had around them, so if they saw a very woolly animal, their first thought wasn't: "Ah, isn't it cute?" It was probably: "Hmm, looks warm, it will make a good sweater." Why is the idea of camel's wool stranger than sheep's wool? (In some parts of the world, sheep's wool may sound weird.) After all, if the material keeps you warm, it's doing its job, right?

What about this one? Gather together all your plastic bags or cookie packages and make yourself a really nice dress or pair of pants. Why is that weird? What do you mean your friends will laugh at you? A lot of the clothes you normally wear use materials such as nylon made from plastic. It's only because the cookie package you think of as food, and material like nylon doesn't feel like plastic.

The kind of things we like as a society changes. Look at the clothes your parents wore when they were young. The style of clothes probably looks a little strange to you now, but for them it was the same style as everyone else. Who knows? In a few years, you could be walking around wearing recycled cookie packages or plastic bags, and it will be perfectly normal.

## ★ Home mission

**Read the statement and make two lists:**

1  I agree with the statement because:

2  I disagree with the statement because:

Spend five minutes writing down as many reasons as you can for both sides of the argument. What do other members of your family think? Did you change your opinion?

**Add your work to the Home mission portfolio.**

> A cheap T-shirt is just as good as an expensive one.

# CONFIDENCE BOOST

Everyone has an opinion when it comes to clothes.

That's just how it goes.

Look in the mirror and ask yourself,

"Am I clean? Do I feel comfortable?"

If the answer is "yes" then you're good to go.

Just remember you're not in any shows.

# WINDOW TO THE WORLD

If it's hot and you're working outside all day, you need some protection from the sun. These conical hats are very popular in many parts of Asia, but especially in Vietnam. They are very practical: they protect you from the sun, but also, because the leaves are waterproof, they are like mini-umbrellas. Some of these hats in Vietnam have a little secret. If you hold them up to the light, you can see a picture or sometimes a poem.

It's a nice idea to have a picture or poem hidden somewhere in your clothes. Why don't you draw a picture or write a few words on a small piece of paper and hide it in your clothes? And don't tell anyone; it's a secret!

# QUIZATHON!

Stopwatches ready! You have 30 seconds per question:

## On your mark, get set, go!

Use the words in the box.

> collar   hat   jewelry   label   raincoat   sleeve
> sneakers   sweater   sweatsuit   tie   tights

1 Which item of clothing rhymes with "my"?

2 Which item of clothing is called *trainers* in the U.K.?

3 Count all the pockets you have today. Don't forget the ones in your backpack.

4 Which of the words from the box are you wearing / do you have today? What about the person who's nearest to you right now?
(Don't look! See if you remember.)

5 Now put them in order of high to low, e.g., *hat* is the highest because it's on your head.

# Video games are bad for you. no, wait, I meant good for you.

"Video games are bad for you." I'm sure you've heard that a few times. Well, if you're playing all day and all night, then it's probably true. It can be very hard to stop: just one more level, just one more life, just five more minutes.

Many kids spend way too much time playing these games. They go to bed late and can't concentrate at school. (I'm sure you don't do that.) If you're having problems sleeping because you're spending too long playing video games, you might need to think about reducing your screen time.

We've all heard the disadvantages, but if I tell you there are advantages, will you believe me?

- Video games can make our brains grow. It's true! There was an experiment where people played a video game for 30 minutes a day. They discovered that the parts of the brain that help you organize your thoughts, know where you are, and make decisions were all bigger.

- They can improve your eyesight. In another experiment, scientists tested the eyesight of their students. They then asked the students to play video games for around ten hours, over a month, and tested their eyesight again. Weirdly, their eyesight was better.

- Wait, there's more! You know when you're playing these games you have to make hundreds of little decisions? If I do this, will I lose a life? If I go straight ahead, I'll have to fight the dragon, etc. It's very simple really: the more decisions you make in the virtual world, the faster you can make decisions in the real world.

So, you see! Gaming is good for you!

**Are the imaginary worlds in books really that different than the imaginary worlds in video games? What do you think? If you play video games, what do you think are some of the advantages?**

## ⭐ Home mission

**Read the statement and make two lists:**

1  I agree with the statement because:

2  I disagree with the statement because:

Spend five minutes writing down as many reasons as you can for both sides of the argument. What do other members of your family think? Did you change your opinion?

**Add your work to the Home mission portfolio.**

Smartphones are making our memories worse.

# WINDOW TO THE WORLD

Can you imagine what it's like to go to a school close to the offices of Apple, Google, or Facebook? The technology must be amazing, right? Not always. There are some schools in the area that have decided to keep the use of technology to an absolute minimum. Instead they encourage students to draw, think, and talk about their school subjects. It's interesting that some of the students' moms and dads probably work in the tech industry, but decided to send their children to a school that uses very little technology.

**What do you think?**

1   Do you want your school to use a lot of tablets and technology, or do you like doing your work with pen and paper?

2   Think of three ways that technology makes your life better.

# CONFIDENCE BOOST

**She's saying all this, he's saying all that.**

**Don't listen to that, just do what you think.**

**She's laughing at him, he's laughing at that.**

**It doesn't mean anything, just do your thing.**

# QUIZATHON!

Many people say that because we use computers and phones so much, we keep less and less information in our heads. Do this test to see how good your memory is:

1   Look at the pictures below for 30 seconds, then close your book and write as many of the objects as you can remember.

How many did you remember? Ask your friends to see how well they did.

2   Try learning the two numbers below: look at each one for ten seconds, then close your book and write them down.

## 7243665

## 392 7048

Which one was easier to remember? Maybe the second one because it was written in chunks? Think about this next time you have to learn a list, a spelling, or a formula.

## 3 Jim-nastics

# Do sports make you smarter?

Everyone says, "Exercise is really good for you." Well, I tested it for myself, and this is my picture diary. Can you match the pictures to the paragraphs?

Doing exercise gives you more energy. It's true! Look, this is me on Monday ① . I spent lunchtime in the library and by two o'clock I couldn't stay awake. But, look at me on Tuesday: at lunchtime I played soccer, and I felt alert all afternoon ② .

I'm taking exams so I need a clear head. It is believed that exercise can help ③ . On the days I felt really tired, I noted how I felt before and after exercise, and I definitely noticed the difference. One day in English, after exercise, my teacher said I was like this ④ because I

answered all the questions. Problem is, the next day, when I didn't exercise, she said my brain was more like this ⑤ .

My dad always says "practice makes perfect". This reminds me of how long it took me to learn to do "kick-ups" ⑥ in soccer practice. When I started, I could only do one or two. Then I practiced for hours and now my record is 53. I learned that playing sports encourages me to keep trying until I succeed ⑦ .

Sports really help my brain as well. I realized that when I'm playing a game, my brain is working really hard. For example, I play soccer and when I control the ball, I make lots of very small movements. I also have to look up and judge the distance between me and the other players, how hard to kick the ball, and so on. I make hundreds of small decisions every time I play. That's great brain exercise ⑧ !

## ★ Home mission

**Read the statement and make two lists:**
1  I agree with the statement because:
2  I disagree with the statement because:

Spend five minutes writing down as many reasons as you can for both sides of the argument. What do other members of your family think? Did you change your opinion?

**Add your work to the Home mission portfolio.**

Sports are a waste of time.

# CONFIDENCE BOOST

Am I going to win the race?

I might, but I'm really not sure.

I could … there's always a chance.

I can! There's no reason I can't.

I will: I practiced hard.

# WINDOW TO THE WORLD

Ever heard of e-sports? No, not two teams chasing after a ball. Instead, it's people sitting and playing video games. Going to a tennis game or soccer game can be exciting, but how do you feel about watching people play e-sports? Yes, that's right: watching people, who are sitting down, staring at a screen, playing a game. Would you believe that roughly 126 million people do exactly that? Yes, 126 million – that's like everyone in Japan watching e-sports.

**What do you think?**

1   Is this how we will all play sports in the future?

2   Are e-sports popular in your country?

**Research the answers to the questions and ask one older person and another person your age for their opinion.**

# QUIZATHON!

Stopwatches ready! You have 30 seconds per question:

## On your mark, get set, go!

1   How many sports can you think of that have seven letters?

2   How many sports can you think of that do not use a ball?

3   What is the longest name of a sport you can think of?

4   Which is the most boring sport in the world?

5   Which is the most exciting?
    (Do your friends agree?)

**Now write three questions to ask your friends.**

## How robot doctors and animals can make you feel better

"How long have you had this pain?"

"Do you have a fever?"

"Does it hurt?"

"Thank you for coming. I hope you're feeling well very soon."

Those sound like the normal type of questions doctors ask you, don't they? But what if this conversation wasn't between you and your doctor? What if you were talking to a robot? What if it was the robot that gave you medicine? What if it was a robot that performed the operation? This isn't something that's going to happen in 50 years' time; it's starting to happen now.

Do you have a pet of any sort? How does it make you feel? Does it make you laugh? If the animal makes you feel good, we often feel better. Dogs are often used in hospitals because they can make some children happier and feel more relaxed. We know that lying in bed all day is not much fun. A dog that wants some attention and becomes your best friend is an excellent way to cheer you up.

However, a hospital needs to be perfectly clean, and animals are not perfectly clean. For this reason, scientists invented the robot Paros the Seal. All it does is look cute – that's it! It has big eyes and moves when you touch it. It knows when you've picked it up, and it knows when it's light and dark. Just by looking cute and responding when you give it attention, it can make you feel better.

### Which statements do you agree/disagree with? Why?

1  Dogs shouldn't be allowed in hospitals.

2  A robot doctor is a cool idea.

3  A robot doctor is a scary idea.

## ⭐ Home mission

**Ask your family:**

1  What do they do when they have a fever?

2  What do they do when they have a cold?

3  Do they have a favorite food or drink for when they're sick?

4  Do they like to be with people, or go to their room and stay in the dark?

5  Do they like other people to look after them, or to be left alone?

**Add your work to the Home mission portfolio.**

# CONFIDENCE BOOST

**Everyone has good days and bad days.**

**Everyone has days when they want to stay in bed.**

**Everyone has days when they feel better.**

**Everyone has days when they feel strong.**

**Everything we do is about learning.**

**Everything we do is about learning to be strong.**

# QUIZATHON!

Find the answers to these questions.

1 What is a normal pulse rate for someone your age?

2 Name two of the four best places to check someone's pulse.

3 What should you do if you think a bone is broken?

4 Which is the largest organ on or in the body?

5 What are your nails made of?

6 What is the name for the holes in your nose?

7 How quickly does information travel along your nerves?

8 You have two lungs and one is bigger than the other. Which one is the biggest?

# WINDOW TO THE WORLD

In rural areas in some countries, it's very difficult to find medicines. People have to travel a long way to towns or cities to get them. It's very hard to travel when you aren't well. For the past few years, a soft drinks company in Zambia has tried to help. When they deliver soft drinks to the rural villages, they also put medicine in the boxes.

Look at a carton of eggs and think about these two questions:

1 What else could you carry in a carton of eggs (without breaking the eggs)?

2 What other uses can you think of for an egg carton?

## 5 Fun foods

# Would you rather have crickets or maggots on your pizza?

**1** ___

Does the idea of eating a cricket make you feel a little sick? Well, get ready, the insects are coming to your plate! There are lots of news stories telling us why we should eat insects. But this isn't new; a quarter of the world's population (around two billion people) already eat insects. Do people eat insects in your country?

**2** ___

The world's population is growing and they all need food. However, some food, like beef, uses a lot of land and water.

You probably use enough water to fill 70 two-liter soda bottles every single day. To produce one kilo of beef, which is enough food for four people, you need 7,700 two-liter bottles.

**3** ___

Why not? They don't look pretty, but a lot of fish don't either. If we look at how much water is used to produce one kilo of insects, that's four soda bottles. It might sound obvious, but cows need a lot of space, insects only need a very small amount. This means we can produce food for a lot of people in a very small space. We also need to remember that

insects are very low in fat and very high in protein, i.e. they're very good for you.

**4** ___

Luckily, there are lots of ways to eat insects; you don't need to crunch on the whole thing. It's very easy to make flour from insects. That way you get lots of wonderful protein in your bread and pizza without having hundreds of little eyes staring at you.

Next time somebody asks you: "Would you prefer beef or chicken?" you know what to say: "A pizza with maggot topping, please."

**Match the heading to the correct paragraph.**

**A** What's the problem?

**B** Do I have to eat the whole thing?

**C** We already eat insects; what are you waiting for?

**D** Why insects?

 **Home mission**

**Show this picture to your family and ask them:**

1 Do people in your country eat insects?
2 Have you ever eaten insects? If yes, describe the taste. If not, would you like to try them?
3 Do you think eating insects will be more popular in the future?
4 Would you rather eat insects or a very smelly cheese?
5 Would you like to try making chocolate-covered crickets?

**Add your work to the Home mission portfolio.**

# CONFIDENCE BOOST

Don't make what you eat a big deal.

If it's insects, vegetables or fish,

Enjoy your next meal.

Make sure you run around and play,

Study, eat, and have fun.

It's the perfect way to spend your day.

# WINDOW TO THE WORLD

Have you ever smelled a really stinky cheese?

That's nothing compared to this stuff called Hákarl from Iceland. You're lucky you can't smell pictures – this one would be really smelly! It is shark that's been buried in sand for about six weeks and then hung to dry for months. It smells truly terrible. When people try it for the first time, they have to hold their nose to stop them from being sick. Hmm, nice.

**What smelly foods can you think of? Put them in order of smelliness.**

# QUIZATHON!

**Try and answer these questions. Then use the Internet to check your answers.**

1 How was the ice pop invented?

   **A** It was invented by a young boy who left a sugary drink and a spoon outside in winter.

   **B** It was invented by an ice cream company.

   **C** It was invented by a mountain climber whose drink froze.

2 This cake is hot on the outside and has ice cream inside. How was it made?

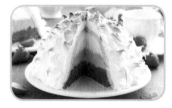

3 Why do onions make you cry?

4 How many bees are needed to make a jar of honey?

## 6 Environmentally friendly

## Cycle power

You wake up in the morning and you turn on the shower. There's lots of hot water for a nice long shower. You want to relax after school, so you turn on the TV and watch your favorite TV shows. Easy, effortless, no pain, no problem.

But your shower and your TV need electricity. Where does this energy come from? Imagine there are 80 people on bikes, next to your house, pedaling really, really, REALLY hard to make the electricity you need. Will that make you a little more careful about the amount of electricity you use?

This is exactly what happened on a television program in the U.K. Cyclists had to generate all the electricity needed in one house by pedaling on bicycles.

When the people in the house needed more electricity, the cyclists pedaled harder and harder.

Do you want a slice of toast? Sure, no problem, you only need ten cyclists: start pedaling. Do you need the microwave? That's another 14 cyclists. And we're not talking about gentle exercise; you need to pedal hard.

Imagine yourself cycling as hard as you can for ten minutes before you can take a shower. Do you think you'll be a little more careful about the electricity you use? When you see just how much energy is needed, you have to rethink the little things we all do every day that just waste energy.

**Think about the questions below:**

1 Think about your morning routine. What things do you turn on and for how long?

2 How many cyclists do you think you need to power your home for your daily breakfast – more or less than 80?

3 Look around your bedroom and complete the sentences using *a lot of*, *a few*, *some* or *many*:

I have _____ electrical things in my bedroom.

I leave _____ electrical things in my bedroom turned on all day.

I leave _____ electrical things in my bedroom turned off all day.

## ⭐ Home mission

**Read the statement and make two lists:**

1 I agree with the statement because:

2 I disagree with the statement because:

Spend five minutes writing down as many reasons as you can for both sides of the argument. What do other members of your family think? Did you change your opinion?

**Add your work to the Home mission portfolio.**

> One person living in an environmentally friendly way doesn't make a difference.

# QUIZATHON!

**What do you think? Research the answers.**

1   Use *a lot of*, *a few*, *some*, *many*. Ask your family to estimate:

How many plastic bags …
- they used last week.
- they reused last week.
- they threw away last week.

2   Keep a record for next week and complete the chart below:

| | How many plastic bags | | |
|---|---|---|---|
| | did you use? | did you reuse? | did you throw away? |
| Sunday | | | |
| Monday | | | |
| Tuesday | | | |
| Wednesday | | | |
| Thursday | | | |
| Friday | | | |
| Saturday | | | |

# WINDOW TO THE WORLD

The Maldives is a group of little islands in the Indian Ocean. In October 2009, its government had a meeting and it was under water! The sea levels are rising and people are very worried that the sea will cover their homes. For many people, climate change causes bigger storms and changes in the weather. But for people in the Maldives, climate change could mean that they lose their homes!

**What do you think?**

1   How did they talk during the meeting?

2   For how long can you hold your breath?

# CONFIDENCE BOOST

Don't worry about what other people do,
You can only control what you do.
Start with something small and very soon,
If everyone follows you,
The world will be as good as new.

## "I'm bored!"
## "That's great news."

Another very busy week! Monday: swimming. Tuesday: I have to go to soccer practice. Wednesday: homework club. Thursday: I should go to my friend's party. Friday: Mom's birthday. Saturday: I have to play in the game. Sunday: I need to stay in bed!

Is that a normal week for you, too? Do you always feel that you have to keep busy? Do you ever feel, well, bored?

Because we are so busy, we think that being bored is a bad thing. We think that if we feel bored, we should be doing something.

We don't like that feeling of time passing, v e r y s l o w l y. Where … one … minute … feels … like … one … hour.

However, scientists say being bored is very good for the brain. Think about it.

When you're bored, what do you do? Don't say "nothing" because that's not true. You probably day-dream, or doodle; generally just let your brain float away.

Do you watch your little brother or sister play? Do they pretend they're an astronaut who has

lost control of their spaceship? Or an explorer saving the life of a dangerous dragon? Or a superhero saving the universe from that same dragon? These are all examples of imaginative play. In each example, the children are solving a (very big) problem. This is really good practice for being an adult. Engineers spend their time fixing problems, doctors try to find out what is making a patient sick, and superheroes need to find ways to save the world. It's good to let your imagination float away, and if you're bored, it should be easy.

So, if you have nothing to do, just sit and enjoy the moment.

**Find the words in the text that mean:**

**A** Think about nothing in particular:

_____

**B** Draw patterns and pictures just for fun:

_____

**C** Opposite of sink:

_____

**D** Opposite of safe:

_____

**E** The part of the brain that can think about things that are not real:

_____

## ⭐ Home mission

**Ask three people in your family the following questions:**

**1** When was the last time you:
- went jogging?
- went on a diet?

**2** How do you keep fit?

**3** What do you do to reduce your stress?

**4** Can you remember the last time you had these emotions?
- amazed       - annoyed
- relaxed       - bored

**5** What happened?

**Add your work to the Home mission portfolio.**

14

# CONFIDENCE BOOST

Take your time, there's time for everything.

Time to eat and time to study, time to watch the snowflakes fall.

Time to swim and time to play, time to do what you want.

Time to sit and think, time to color in, and time to be bored.

## WINDOW TO THE WORLD

Have you seen patterns like the one below? They have become very popular with adults (and children). Modern life can be very busy, especially in cities: lots of noise, traffic, people everywhere. Just sitting, coloring, not thinking about anything, sounds nice, doesn't it? It's very relaxing. Why don't you try it? See if anyone in your family wants to join you.

Get some pencils, ask your family to join you and start coloring. Take your time and don't think about anything. Careful, once you start you won't be able to stop!

## QUIZATHON!

Remember, feeling bored can help you be more creative. Here's a collection of strange questions. Just answer what feels right.

1 Do you think you are more like a square or a circle?

2 How many uses can you think of for a paper cup?

3 What do you think flowers talk about?

4 What might happen if all the computers stop working at the same time?

5 Can you play tennis with a square ball?

6 Imagine you can talk to animals. What will you ask them?

And now, how do you feel? Still bored? Relaxed? Amazed? ... Next time you feel bored you can think about questions like these!

## History is now!

Did you use to get bored when your parents took you sightseeing? That's OK, it's normal. But maybe these glasses will make it more exciting. Put them on and let's try something new!

First stop, the Natural History Museum. You walk through the doors and see a huge skeleton of a blue whale, but wait, what's happening? It's moving! It's real! It's in the water. Suddenly, you see its huge body jumping out of the water, and now you're very wet. You take off your glasses, but the skeleton is still there. It hasn't moved.

Now, the History Museum. Look at that huge block of stone that used to be part of the pyramids in Egypt.

How did they move something so big and heavy? Hey, who are all these men? What are they doing? Let's use the glasses and find out. There are lots of men. They're pulling the stones through the sand. They don't have any machines. The first man is splashing water on the sand. Why? Ah, it's easier to pull the stone on wet sand than on dry sand. It looks like very hard work.

Maybe a little art? Look at possibly the most famous painting in the world: the *Mona Lisa*. Who's that? It's Leonardo da Vinci and he's painting the *Mona Lisa*. Let's get closer. Hmm, he doesn't look happy. What's the problem? Oh, look, he's painting over the smile. He's doing it again. He wants it to be perfect.

What do you think? Would that make sightseeing more interesting for you? Well, it's probably not too far in the future.

**Think about these questions:**

1   Would you rather go to a museum using these glasses or go to an amusement park? Why?

2   Can you think of any things or places you'd like to see using these glasses?

## ⭐ Home mission

**Read the statement and make two lists:**

1   I agree with the statement because:

2   I disagree with the statement because:

Spend five minutes writing down as many reasons as you can for both sides of the argument. What do other members of your family think? Did you change your opinion?

**Add your work to the Home mission portfolio.**

> Now that we have all the information we need on the Internet, we don't need museums any more.

# WINDOW TO THE WORLD

Do you think art galleries are not very exciting? What about if you had to swim underwater to see the exhibits? That art museum exists. It's called MUSA and is in Mexico. The sculptures and the whole collection is eight meters underwater. The idea of the museum is very simple: see statues of people doing normal things in a very unusual place – underwater. All the statues are covered with seaweed. This makes the museum feel very strange; it's like time has stopped.

**Find out about these museums. Would you like to visit them? Why or why not?**

● The Gnome Reserve, Devon, U.K.

● The Wallpaper Museum, Rixheim, France

● Museum Cemento, Rezola, Spain

## QUIZATHON!

**Find out a little about what people used to do in your town.**

1 Find two big buildings that used to be something different.

2 Where did people use to go for a walk one hundred years ago?

3 Where did people use to go shopping one hundred years ago?

4 Does your town have a movie theater now? Did it use to have one a hundred years ago?

## CONFIDENCE BOOST

There's a whole wide world out there.

Maybe I'll get to see it one day.

It's a thought that's not so rare.

Maybe there is a way, one day.

But if you close your eyes,

You can see the whole world in your head.

And you can do it every day!

You'll see it's a fun way!

## Animation

When we look around, we see people moving, we see cars driving past, so why are we so amazed by animation?

### How does animation work?

When your eye sees something, it holds on to the picture for much less than a second and then looks at the next one. If you see lots of pictures, one after the other very quickly, then your poor brain gets confused. It thinks the pictures are moving. Wave your hand as quickly as you can in front of your face. What do you see? Try it in front of a TV screen. Now what do you see?

### How many frames do you need to make a movie?

Now, let's do some math. To confuse your brain, you need 24 separate pictures every second. That's fast. That means that an artist needs to draw 24 slightly different pictures to get one second of animation.

To get an idea of the speed, see how fast you can tap your finger on the table. Maybe around ten times a second? Try it: search for "Click-speed test" online.

### Getting things right

If you're making a movie with hundreds of thousands of frames, then you don't want it to be full of mistakes. Movie studios spend a lot of time talking about only a few seconds of work. (Remember, one second is 24 pictures.) If they have to start again, they will. For example, every morning at the Pixar studios, they watch the animation from the day before and discuss how to make it even better. This means that a lot of lhe pictures the artists draw aren't used.

It's a hard lesson to learn, but you're not throwing away everything you learned, you're using it to make something even better.

Think about it a little. The animators are drawing very complicated scenes with lots of characters and movement. Each picture takes a lot of work to change.

### How many pictures does an artist need for one minute? (Hint: multiply seconds in a minute by 24.)

1 second = 24 pictures

1 minute (60 seconds) = _____ pictures

60 minutes = 86,400 pictures

90 minutes = _____ pictures (Can you do this one without a calculator?)

### Make your own animation

Get a fairly thick book and in the bottom corner draw your animation frames, for example, a dog chasing a cat. Then as you flick through the pages, the animation will come to life. Or maybe you can create your own animation on a computer?

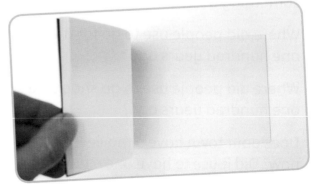

**If you were a movie star …**

**Ask your family:**

1 What kind of movies would you make?
2 Would you like photographers taking pictures of you?
3 Would you have your house redecorated or would you buy a bigger house?
4 Would you still have the same friends?
5 Would you make movies in English?

**Add your work to the Home mission portfolio.**

 **QUIZATHON!**

Use the Internet and find out what these jobs in the film industry are:

1 gaffer
2 boom operator
3 best boy
4 data wrangler
5 prop maker

Would you like to do any of these jobs?

 **WINDOW TO THE WORLD**

You've definitely heard of Hollywood. You may have heard of Bollywood – the Indian film industry. But have you ever heard about Nollywood – the Nigerian film industry?

Hollywood makes the most money and its movies are popular all over the world, but Nollywood makes more movies and its heroines and heroes are often more famous than Hollywood stars throughout Africa. In the past, the quality of Nollywood films wasn't very good, but they were very cheap for people to buy. Now, the quality is getting a lot better with better performances from the actors and more money spent on the scenes.

**Now think about these questions:**

1 Does your country have a big film industry?
2 Do you like movies made in your country?
3 Are they popular in other countries?
4 When was the last time you went to the movie theater to watch a movie made in your country?

**CONFIDENCE BOOST**

Fall down seven times, get up eight.

What do you think this means? Is that what you do?

| Word | Topic | Part of speech | Example sentence | A similar word? |
|---|---|---|---|---|
| sneakers | Clothes Sports | noun | He has some expensive sneakers. | shoes |
| | | | | |
| | | | | |
| | | | | |
| | | | | |
| | | | | |
| | | | | |
| | | | | |
| | | | | |
| | | | | |
| | | | | |

**CHALLENGE**

Say three clothes words that start with the letter "t"!

| Word | Topic | Part of speech | Example sentence | A similar word? |
|------|-------|----------------|------------------|-----------------|
|      |       |                |                  |                 |
|      |       |                |                  |                 |
|      |       |                |                  |                 |
|      |       |                |                  |                 |
|      |       |                |                  |                 |
|      |       |                |                  |                 |
|      |       |                |                  |                 |
|      |       |                |                  |                 |
|      |       |                |                  |                 |
|      |       |                |                  |                 |

**CHALLENGE**

Close your eyes and spell one technology word backwards in ten seconds!

| Word | Topic | Part of speech | Example sentence | A similar word? |
|------|-------|----------------|------------------|-----------------|
|      |       |                |                  |                 |
|      |       |                |                  |                 |
|      |       |                |                  |                 |
|      |       |                |                  |                 |
|      |       |                |                  |                 |
|      |       |                |                  |                 |
|      |       |                |                  |                 |
|      |       |                |                  |                 |
|      |       |                |                  |                 |
|      |       |                |                  |                 |
|      |       |                |                  |                 |

**CHALLENGE**

Draw three sports words in one picture!

| Word | Topic | Part of speech | Example sentence | A similar word? |
|------|-------|----------------|------------------|-----------------|
|      |       |                |                  |                 |
|      |       |                |                  |                 |
|      |       |                |                  |                 |
|      |       |                |                  |                 |
|      |       |                |                  |                 |
|      |       |                |                  |                 |
|      |       |                |                  |                 |
|      |       |                |                  |                 |
|      |       |                |                  |                 |
|      |       |                |                  |                 |

**CHALLENGE**

How many new words can you make from the letters in "emergency services"?

| Word | Topic | Part of speech | Example sentence | A similar word? |
|------|-------|----------------|------------------|-----------------|
|      |       |                |                  |                 |
|      |       |                |                  |                 |
|      |       |                |                  |                 |
|      |       |                |                  |                 |
|      |       |                |                  |                 |
|      |       |                |                  |                 |
|      |       |                |                  |                 |
|      |       |                |                  |                 |
|      |       |                |                  |                 |
|      |       |                |                  |                 |

**CHALLENGE**

Say the three different food words that we spell with: two letter "c"s, two letter "b"s, and two letter "o"s!

| Word | Topic | Part of speech | Example sentence | A similar word? |
|------|-------|----------------|------------------|-----------------|
|      |       |                |                  |                 |
|      |       |                |                  |                 |
|      |       |                |                  |                 |
|      |       |                |                  |                 |
|      |       |                |                  |                 |
|      |       |                |                  |                 |
|      |       |                |                  |                 |
|      |       |                |                  |                 |
|      |       |                |                  |                 |
|      |       |                |                  |                 |

**CHALLENGE**

Write down as many environmentally friendly words as you can in one minute!

| Word | Topic | Part of speech | Example sentence | A similar word? |
|------|-------|----------------|------------------|-----------------|
|      |       |                |                  |                 |
|      |       |                |                  |                 |
|      |       |                |                  |                 |
|      |       |                |                  |                 |
|      |       |                |                  |                 |
|      |       |                |                  |                 |
|      |       |                |                  |                 |
|      |       |                |                  |                 |
|      |       |                |                  |                 |
|      |       |                |                  |                 |

**CHALLENGE**

Use as many feelings words as you can in your next English class. Keep count!

| Word | Topic | Part of speech | Example sentence | A similar word? |
|------|-------|----------------|------------------|-----------------|
|      |       |                |                  |                 |
|      |       |                |                  |                 |
|      |       |                |                  |                 |
|      |       |                |                  |                 |
|      |       |                |                  |                 |
|      |       |                |                  |                 |
|      |       |                |                  |                 |
|      |       |                |                  |                 |
|      |       |                |                  |                 |
|      |       |                |                  |                 |

**CHALLENGE**

Say all the capital cities you know in English in one minute!

| Word | Topic | Part of speech | Example sentence | A similar word? |
|---|---|---|---|---|
| | | | | |
| | | | | |
| | | | | |
| | | | | |
| | | | | |
| | | | | |
| | | | | |
| | | | | |
| | | | | |
| | | | | |

**CHALLENGE**

Group the TV and movie words you know by their word stress! How many stress patterns are there?

| | The most important things I learned | What I most want to remember | What I need to learn more about |
|---|---|---|---|
| Unit 1 | | | |
| Unit 2 | | | |
| Unit 3 | | | |

| | The most important things I learned | What I most want to remember | What I need to learn more about |
|---|---|---|---|
| Unit 4 | | | |
| Unit 5 | | | |
| Unit 6 | | | |

|  | The most important things I learned | What I most want to remember | What I need to learn more about |
|---|---|---|---|
| Unit 7 |  |  |  |
| Unit 8 |  |  |  |
| Unit 9 |  |  |  |